U.S. NAVY SEALs
IT'S NOT JUST A GAME
www.seal.navy.mil

SOCOM
U.S. NAVY SEALS

PRIMA'S OFFICIAL STRATEGY GUIDE

GREG OFF

Prima Games
A Division of Random House, Inc.

3000 Lava Ridge Court, Roseville, CA 95661 — (916) 787-7000
www.primagames.com

Layout and design: Tim Lindquist

™ The Premier Series logo is a trademark of Dimension Publishing, Inc.

ISBN: 0-7615-3691-4
Library of Congress Catalog Card Number: 2002-109756
Printed in the United States of America

03 04 XX 10 9 8 7 6 5 4

Welcome to the SOCOM: U.S. Navy SEALs Official Strategy Guide. This guide is written and designed as a tactical aid, giving you and your SEAL team members the vital information you need before heading out onto the virtual battlefield. We have broken the guide down into several sections, with the bulk of it focusing on the 12 Single-Player missions. Each mission has its own set of Primary and Secondary Objectives for which we offer detailed strategies. We have tried to make the guide as versatile as possible, allowing you to either use it as a straight-forward walkthrough or, for those of you who might only want help from time-to-time, as a companion when you just might need a little help achieving a certain mission objective. Either way, this guide provides you with all of the tools you need to get the job done. Good luck, SEALs, we're counting on you.

TABLE OF CONTENTS

BOOT CAMP

MEET YOUR SEAL TEAM MEMBERS:
SEALs always travel in tight-knit Fire Teams and yours is no different. Your Team is comprised of two Elements: Able and Bravo -- each made up of two team members. You (call sign Kahuna) and your partner, Hutchins (call sign Boomer), are in the Able Element and Bailey (call sign Spectre) and Dimone (call sign Jester) make up Bravo Element. On the battlefield, you can split up the two Elements, but SEAL SOP (standard operating procedure) dictates you always stay with your assigned SEAL partner. In this case, Boomer will always be by your side, and Spectre and Jester will always stay together.

SEAL MOVEMENT AND ACTIONS:

CONTROLLER CONFIGURATIONS:
When you first boot up SOCOM: U.S. Navy SEALs, you will be given the choice of two controller configurations: Sure Shot and Precision Shooter. There are an additional two: Scout and Lefty, available via the Options Menu under the Controller Presets option. For the purpose of the guide, we have written it using the Precision Shooter control option. For more information and breakdowns of the other configurations, see the game's instruction manual or check them out via the Controller Preset option on the Options Menu

QUICK REFERENCE CONTROLLER CONFIGURATION -- PRECISION SHOOTER:

Start button = Pause
Select button = TACMAP Objectives
Directional Pad:
Left - Right = Peek
Up = Change Perspective, Zoom Sniper Scope, Binoculars, Nightvision Goggles
Down = Change Perspective, Zoom out
Left Analog Stick = Character Movement up/down, Strafe left/right
Press L3 = Change Fire Rate
Right Analog Stick = Aim Weapon, Rotate Character left/right
Press R3 = Reload
□ = Jump
✕ = Execute Special Action
◎ = Issue Commands
△ = Change Stance
L1 = Primary Weapon Quick Select
L2 = Secondary Weapon Quick Select
R1 = Fire Weapon, Throw Grenade
R2 = Activate Weapons Cache

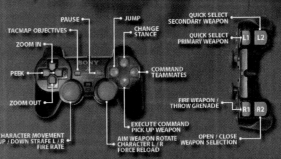

MOVING KAHUNA:
The left analog stick moves Kahuna in any given direction. It is pressure sensitive, meaning the more you press the stick, the faster Kahuna will travel. Also, if you press the stick lightly in any given direction, he will walk very slowly. It is very important in the game to use stealth to your advantage, so you will need to master moving slowly and methodically if you want to succeed in your missions.

AIMING WEAPONS AND LOOKING:

The right analog stick is used to manually aim the current weapon you have selected, as well as to look around. Aiming is carried out using the on-screen cross hairs. To aim at an enemy, just point the cross hairs over your target. The default mode for aiming and looking (pitch) is pressing up on the stick to aim/look upwards and down on the stick to aim/look downwards. It's possible to Invert and reverse the pitch via the Pause Screen under the Invert Pitch option. To access the Pause Screen press the Start button during gameplay.

CROSS HAIRS AND TARGETING:

Your cross hairs will change color from yellow to red when you have an enemy in your sights. The color yellow indicates that you don't have an enemy targeted, or that you can't shoot the enemy from your vantage point. Sometimes he might be out of targeting range and, even though your cross hairs are directly over your target, he is too far away to be hit. Red cross hairs indicate that the enemy is targeted and you will be able to hit them. If you have Assisted Aiming turned on (accessible via the pause screen), you will see a second, red-colored square targeting reticle appear over your targeted enemy. As long as the reticle stays on your targeted enemy, your weapon will be "locked on" to him, guaranteeing a direct hit to the body. If there is an obstacle or obstruction in your path, such as a fence railing, tree, wall, etc., you will get a red-colored circle with a line through it, indicating that the targeted enemy can't be hit. Lastly, your cross hairs will turn green when you aim them at a friendly (such as a fellow SEAL team member, hostage, or a surrendering enemy).

CHANGING BODY POSITION:

There are three positions you can assume: Stand, Crouch and Prone -- each necessary to achieve your objectives. When standing, you are most vulnerable and can easily be seen by the enemy, but you can quickly run and maneuver. Crouching allows you to slowly walk in a crouched position, making it harder to be seen. It also gives you the ability to duck down and take cover behind objects. This position is quite useful and should be used in most situations. The Prone position allows you to get down on your belly and crawl. Crawling is useful when you want to avoid the enemy's line of sight or hide in foliage. It is also the most stable position from which to shoot, giving you much better control and precision over your shots. You can cycle through each position by pressing the ▲ Button. It is also possible to quickly skip one position to get into another by double tapping the ▲ button. For example, if you want to go from a Stand to the Prone position quickly, just double tap on the ▲ button.

JUMPING:

You can execute a short jump by pressing the ⬜ button. Jumping is useful when you need to hop over small objects or ledges quickly, instead of using the Climb option.

PEEKING:

Peeking around corners is a very useful tool and must be used if you intend to be successful in your missions. Peeking allows you to stay in the relative safety of cover, such as behind objects or corners, while still being able to survey the area or target an enemy. You can Peek from any position (Stand, Crouch or Prone), by pressing right or left on the directional button.

CHANGING PERSPECTIVES:

There are multiple perspectives in the game, including third and first-person, as well as levels of zoom (depending on whether you are using a scope-equipped rifle or Binoculars and Nightvision Goggles). To change perspectives, press up on the directional button. The default perspective is third-person, but you can always access the first-person perspective by pressing up on the directional button. If you have Binoculars, Nightvision Goggles or a scope-equipped rifle, pressing up on the directional button a second time will switch to that perspective.

WEAPONS:

There are many different kinds of weapons you can wield in the game, including Primary and Secondary weapons (rifles and machine guns, and pistols), as well as explosive devices (grenades, mines, C-4 charges, etc.). You can change weapons for the whole team, each Element, or individual SEAL team members before heading into a mission via the Armory screen. For the purposes of this guide, we have written it using the default equipment the game automatically issues you based on SOP (standard operating procedure) and the current tactical evaluation for each mission. Be advised, using an improper weapon may compromise your objectives and result in mission failure. In addition to your Primary and Secondary weapons, you will always carry a combat knife as well.

FIRING/THROWING/DEPLOYING WEAPONS:
When you have a weapon equipped, such as a rifle, pistol, grenade or C-4 charge, you can fire, throw or deploy it by pressing the `R1` button. Some weapons, such as grenades, are pressure sensitive, meaning that the harder you press down on the `R1` button, the further it will travel in the air.

SWITCHING BETWEEN PRIMARY AND SECONDARY WEAPONS:
You automatically carry Primary (rifle) and Secondary (pistol) weapons. You can only carry one of each at a time, meaning that if you want to pick up a fallen enemy's weapon, you will have to trade it for yours. You can switch between your Primary and Secondary weapons by pressing the `L1` and `L2` buttons. The `L1` button is assigned to your Primary weapon and the `L2` button is assigned to your Secondary weapon. It is also possible to reassign these buttons for other weapons in your Weapons Cache. To do so, press the `R2` button to pull up your Weapons Cache, cycle through your available equipment and highlight the one you want using the directional button, and then press either the `L1` or `L2` button to map that button to the weapon. The words "Quick 1" and "Quick 2" will appear over the weapon you have selected.

SETTING YOUR WEAPON'S FIRE MODE:

Many assault weapons have multiple firing modes, allowing you to change the rate of fire from single shot to burst. Depending on the weapon you are carrying, you can set it up to a five shot burst. To switch firing modes, press down on the L3 button (the left analog stick). The Bullet icon on the Weapon in Hand display in the left corner of the screen will change from one to three (burst) or more (for fully automatic weapons, such as the M4A1 SD).

RELOADING:

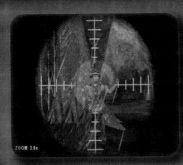

Both your rifle and pistol carry a finite amount of ammo before their chambers/cartridges/magazines become empty. You can quickly reload anytime during gameplay by pressing down on the R3 button (the right analog stick). The current weapon you have equipped, along with the number of shots remaining in the magazine, maximum rounds available per magazine, and the amount of ammunition remaining are displayed in the Current Weapon menu located in the bottom left corner of the screen.

SNIPER RIFLES:

Sniper rifles are designed to hit a long-range target with precision. You can zoom in or out on the target via the rifle's scope by pressing up on the directional button. Some sniper rifles have multiple levels of zoom, which can be accessed by pressing up a second time. To exit out of the sniper mode, press the directional button down. When aiming with your scope, you will have to take into account the adrenaline coursing through your veins. In these tense situations your heart will beat faster than normal and you might have a harder time keeping your sights trained on your target. When aiming your scope at an enemy, make slow, precise movements and give yourself a moment to calm down before adjusting your aim. Sniper rifles do not handle well in a close-range firefight.

THE WEAPONS CACHE:

You can pull up your Weapons Cache by pressing the R2 button during gameplay. This pulls up an on-screen sub-menu with which you can cycle through your available inventory by pressing up or down on the directional button. When you have highlighted the item you want to select, press the Action (X) button to equip it. In this mode, you can select other equipment and items, such as explosive devices, as well as assign Quick buttons for your Primary and Secondary weapons (see Switching Between Primary and Secondary Weapons above for more details).

SILENT KILLS:

There will be many times where stealth will be required in order to fulfill a mission objective. When stealth is needed, the most silent attacks involve hand-to-hand combat tactics. Whenever possible, it's highly recommended you use a well-placed rifle butt to an enemy's head, or stab him with your combat knife. These moves can be executed by silently moving right next to the enemy, preferably from behind and in the standing position, and then pressing the Attack (R1) button when the corresponding icon appears on-screen. Both rifle butt strikes and knife attacks can be performed on surrendering or restrained enemies.

WEAPONS AND EQUIPMENT LIST:

PISTOLS

PISTOL: 226

VOLUME	
ACCURACY	
RANGE	
FIRE RATE	
FIRE MODES	SINGLE

PISTOL: DE .50

VOLUME	
ACCURACY	
RANGE	
FIRE RATE	
FIRE MODES	SINGLE

PISTOL: F57

VOLUME	
ACCURACY	
RANGE	
FIRE RATE	
FIRE MODES	SINGLE

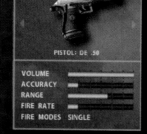

PISTOL: M9

VOLUME	
ACCURACY	
RANGE	
FIRE RATE	
FIRE MODES	SINGLE

PISTOL: MARK 23

VOLUME	
ACCURACY	
RANGE	
FIRE RATE	
FIRE MODES	SINGLE

SILENCED PISTOL: MARK 23 SD

VOLUME	
ACCURACY	
RANGE	
FIRE RATE	
FIRE MODES	SINGLE

AUTOMATIC PISTOL: MODEL 18

VOLUME	
ACCURACY	
RANGE	
FIRE RATE	
FIRE MODES	SINGLE-BURST-AUTO

SILENCED PISTOL: 9MM PISTOL

VOLUME	
ACCURACY	
RANGE	
FIRE RATE	
FIRE MODES	SINGLE

CARBINES

RIFLE: AKS-74

VOLUME	
ACCURACY	
RANGE	
FIRE RATE	
FIRE MODES	SINGLE-BURST-AUTO

RIFLE: AK-47

VOLUME	
ACCURACY	
RANGE	
FIRE RATE	
FIRE MODES	SINGLE-BURST-AUTO

RIFLE: AKS-74

VOLUME	
ACCURACY	
RANGE	
FIRE RATE	
FIRE MODES	SINGLE-BURST-AUTO

ASSAULT RIFLE: 552

VOLUME	
ACCURACY	
RANGE	
FIRE RATE	
FIRE MODES	SINGLE-BURST-AUTO

SUBMACHINE GUN: HK5

VOLUME	
ACCURACY	
RANGE	
FIRE RATE	
FIRE MODES	SINGLE-BURST-AUTO

SUBMACHINE GUN: HK5 SD

VOLUME	
ACCURACY	
RANGE	
FIRE RATE	
FIRE MODES	SINGLE-BURST-AUTO

ASSAULT RIFLE: M4A1

VOLUME	
ACCURACY	
RANGE	
FIRE RATE	
FIRE MODES	SINGLE-BURST-AUTO

ASSAULT RIFLE: M4A1 SD

VOLUME	
ACCURACY	
RANGE	
FIRE RATE	
FIRE MODES	SINGLE-BURST-AUTO

ASSAULT RIFLE: M4A1-M203

VOLUME	
ACCURACY	
RANGE	
FIRE RATE	
FIRE MODES	SINGLE-BURST-AUTO

RIFLE: M14

VOLUME	
ACCURACY	
RANGE	
FIRE RATE	
FIRE MODES	SINGLE-AUTO

RIFLE: M16A2

VOLUME	
ACCURACY	
RANGE	
FIRE RATE	
FIRE MODES	SINGLE-BURST

RIFLE: M16A2-M203

VOLUME	
ACCURACY	
RANGE	
FIRE RATE	
FIRE MODES	SINGLE-BURST

CARBINES

MACHINE GUN: M60E3

VOLUME	
ACCURACY	
RANGE	
FIRE RATE	
FIRE MODES	AUTO

MACHINE GUN: M63A

VOLUME	
ACCURACY	
RANGE	
FIRE RATE	
FIRE MODES	SINGLE-BURST-AUTO

GRENADE LAUNCHER: M79

VOLUME	
ACCURACY	
RANGE	
FIRE RATE	
FIRE MODES	SINGLE

SUBMACHINE GUN: F90

VOLUME	
ACCURACY	
RANGE	
FIRE RATE	
FIRE MODES	SINGLE-BURST-AUTO

SNIPER RIFLES

SNIPER RIFLE: M40A1

VOLUME	
ACCURACY	
RANGE	
FIRE RATE	
FIRE MODES	SINGLE

SNIPER RIFLE: M82A1A

VOLUME	
ACCURACY	
RANGE	
FIRE RATE	
FIRE MODES	SINGLE

SNIPER RIFLE: M87ELR

VOLUME	
ACCURACY	
RANGE	
FIRE RATE	
FIRE MODES	SINGLE

SNIPER RIFLE: SR-25

VOLUME	
ACCURACY	
RANGE	
FIRE RATE	
FIRE MODES	SINGLE

SNIPER RIFLE: SR-25 SD

VOLUME	
ACCURACY	
RANGE	
FIRE RATE	
FIRE MODES	SINGLE

EQUIPMENT

GRENADE: AN-M8

Creates a large cloud of white smoke when activated, which can be used for signalling other units and screening movement.

EXPLOSIVE: C4

Plastic demolition explosive, made of volatile chemicals and plasticizer, that can be molded into varying shapes.

MINE: CLAYMORE

A lethal anti-personnel weapon, the Claymore fires a cloud of small, shot-like pellets through the air when detonated by the player.

EQUIPMENT: DOUBLE AMMO

This auxiliary item increases the number of rounds for the player's primary and secondary weapons.

GRENADE: HE

The damage from a HE grenade is caused by the concussive force of the explosion, which allows destruction of objects as well as enemy personnel.

GRENADE: M67

This powerful grenade sends a blast of shrapnel hurling outward from the explosion, making it a deadly area-effect weapon.

GRENADE: M79 FRAG ROUND (6)

A fragmentation grenade fired from the M79 grenade launcher.

GRENADE: M79 HE ROUND (6)

A high-explosive grenade fired from the M79 grenade launcher.

GRENADE: M79 SMOKE ROUND (3)

A smoke grenade used to provide cover for unit movement; fired from the M79 grenade launcher.

GRENADE: M203 FRAG ROUND (6)

This is a fragmentation grenade fired from the M203 grenade launcher.

GRENADE: M203 HE ROUND (6)

A high-explosive round, fired from the M203 grenade launcher, that does damage to material and people.

GRENADE: M203 SMOKE ROUND (3)

A smoke grenade, used to provide cover for troop movement, which is fired from the M203 grenade launcher.

GRENADE: MARK141

A non-lethal grenade designed to incapacitate its target through blinding light and loud noise. Also known as a stun grenade.

EXPLOSIVE: SATCHEL CHARGE

A charge composed of blocks of explosive wired together in order to produce a single, powerful explosion.

SPECIAL ACTIONS:

There will be many times throughout each mission where Special Actions will be required. Special Actions can vary from climbing and opening doors to picking up weapons and items and moving bodies. When a Special Action is required, a Special Action Icon will appear in the bottom-center of the screen. When you want to perform a Special Action, press the Action (✗) button when the icon appears. If multiple Special Actions are available at the same time (such as moving a body and picking up a weapon), press and hold the Action (✗) button and press the directional pad left and right to cycle through the icons. When you have the one you want, release the button to execute the Special Action. In addition to displaying the icons below, we have placed them in the body of the guide to give you a visual reference when you should be executing a command or Special Action.

 ORDER ICON:
This is the most common icon you will see during the course of the game. It will appear when you issue a command to your SEAL team members, a hostage, escortee or restrainee. To learn more about issuing commands using the SOCOM Headset or button controls, see the Issuing Commands section below. When this icon appears over a hostage, escortee or restrainee, press the Action (✗) button to either order them to "Hold Position" or "Follow."

 LADDER SLIDE ICON:
To get down a ladder quickly, press the Action (✗) button when this icon appears.

 OPEN AND CLOSE DOOR ICONS:
These icons will appear when you approach a closed or open door. A little known secret: You can kick open a door if you hold down the Action (✗) button before you approach the door and release it when the icon appears.

 FLIP SWITCH ICONS:
These icons will appear when there is a piece of equipment to turn on or off. Certain missions will entail the operation or disabling of equipment, such as radio comm units, generators, batteries, etc. When you come across a piece of equipment, approach it for the icon to appear.

 DISABLE ICON:
There will be certain scenarios in SOCOM where you will need to disable a piece of machinery or disarm a bomb. When you find the item you need to disable, point your cross hairs over it until this icon appears. Press the Action (✗) button to execute the move.

 PICK UP BODY ICON:
Dead bodies are a dead giveaway, betraying your presence if they are spotted by an enemy. When stealth is your primary goal, it's best to pick up a fallen foe and move them to an area out of the enemy line of sight (such as behind a stack of crates), or one that is in complete darkness. To pick up a dead body, position yourself either on top of it or right next to it until the "Pick Up Body" icon appears and press the Action (✗) button. You can then slowly walk with a dead body and move it to a secure area. To drop the body, simply press the Action (✗) button once again. You can not shoot while holding a body.

 RESTRAIN ICON:
This icon appears when either an enemy has surrendered (by dropping his weapon and throwing up his hands), or when you need to restrain a hostage or friendly (SOP). The Restrain icon will only appear when you are right behind the target. Certain missions will require you to secure a target by restraining them, and then extracting them out of the area. If the Voice icon appears once they have been restrained, you will be able to order them to "Follow" or "Hold Position."

 SILENT KILL ICONS:
When these icons appear, you can execute a quick and deadly Silent Kill (see Silent Kills above for more information).

 CLIMBING ICONS:
The Climb icon will appear whenever you come to an obstacle that you can climb on, such as crates, ledges, ladders, etc. To climb up onto small objects, press the Action (✗) button when the icon appears. To climb up on larger/higher objects, such as high ledges and ladders, press the Action (✗) button when the icon appears and then press up and down on the directional button.

 EXPLOSIVE ICONS:
There will be times when you need to place an explosive device, such as a satchel or C-4 charge, on an object or obstruction. To do so, walk up to the object you want to blow up and press the Action (✗) button when this icon appears.

PICK UP ICON:
There are certain items you will be required to retrieve during your missions. When you come across an item, the Pick Up icon will appear. Press the Action (✗) button item to pick it up.

 TAKE WEAPON ICONS:
You can swap out both your Primary and Secondary weapons with a fallen foe's at any time. While most of the time you should stick with what you have brought into the mission, there will be instances when you are running low or out of ammunition and need another weapon to continue. To trade weapons, position yourself over the dropped weapon on the ground. When "Take Weapon" icon appears, press the Action (✗) button to drop yours and replace it with the other.

ISSUING COMMANDS:

Teamwork and using your fellow SEAL team members is the key to success in SOCOM. The only way to work together with your teammates is to issue commands. There are two ways of issuing commands, either using voice commands via the Headset bundled with the game, or using button controls. A command has three components: WHO, WHAT, and either WHERE or HOW, and you can string a command together by combining these components. To execute a command, you must use the Command (◉) button, which will activate the Voice Command menu.

USING THE HEADSET:

Your Headset gives you voice contact with your team to issue commands, as well as keeps you informed on the tactical situation from each team member and SOCOM HQ. To use the Headset to issue commands, press and hold the ◉ button, which activates the Voice Command menu. Now, speak into the microphone attached to the Headset and say the WHO, WHAT and WHERE or HOW in the form of an unbroken sentence. For example, pressing the Command (◉) button and saying "Team (WHO), Fire At Will (WHAT)," will tell your fellow SEAL team members to take any and every open shot. You will get a verbal response if they acknowledge your order. Speaking clearly and loudly will give you the best results.

USING BUTTON CONTROLS:

Commands can be issued using menu selections via the Voice Command menu as an alternative to the Headset, or as a way to learn and memorize the commands. To open the Voice Command menu, tap the Command (◉) button once. This opens up the first (WHO) menu. Select who you want to command by pressing the directional pad up or down and then press the Action (✖) button to confirm. This will open up the second (WHAT) sub menu. If you choose a command that has a WHERE or HOW -- for example: "Bravo (WHO), Lead to (WHAT) Cross hairs (WHERE)" -- a third sub menu will open up. Pressing the Action (✖) button confirms the command and your team members will execute your orders.

COMMAND DESCRIPTIONS:

WHO:

Team: Saying or choosing "Team" will give the order to both Able and Bravo.
Able: Saying or choosing "Able" will give an order specifically to Boomer.
Bravo: Saying or choosing "Bravo" will give an order specifically to Bravo Element (Jester and Spectre).
Escortee: The Escortee command will only become available if you have someone in custody. Saying or choosing "Escortee" will give an order specifically to the Escortee and is typically only "Follow" or "Hold Position" (note: your cross hairs must be pointed at a potential escortee for the command header to appear in the Voice Command menu.)
Support: The Support command will only be available on certain missions. Calling in support will bring in your support helicopter, which can sweep in and provide cover fire or pick up and extract an escortee.

COMMAND DESCRIPTIONS:

WHAT:

Hold Fire: Saying or choosing "Hold Fire" will command your team members to shoot only when shot at.

Fire At Will: Saying or choosing "Fire At Will" will command your team members to take any and every open shot.

Cover Area: Saying or choosing "Cover Area" will order your team members to provide covering fire at the area you are pointing your cross hairs. This command is helpful when you want to guard a doorway or protect an escortee.

Deploy: Saying or choosing "Deploy" will order your team members to throw or place an explosive at the area you are pointing your cross hairs. The Deploy command is used in conjunction with the WHERE or HOW commands.

Ambush: Saying or choosing "Ambush" will order your team members to remove any hostiles in the immediate area. This command is especially useful in wide open, exterior areas.

Run To: Saying or choosing "Run To" will command your team to move out to a specific location. The Run To command is used in conjunction with the WHERE commands. Each mission has specific Navigation Points (Nav points) that are prese-lected before going in. These are labeled on your TACMAP (see TACMAP for more information).

Lead To: Saying or choosing "Lead To" will command your team to escort you to a specific location. They will take the lead and you can follow behind. The Lead To command is also used in conjunction with the WHERE commands.

Attack To: Saying or choosing "Attack To" will order your team to take all available shots while moving to a specific loca-tion. The Attack To command is also used in conjunction with the WHERE commands.

Stealth To: Saying or choosing "Stealth To" will command your team to use shadow and coverage while moving to a spe-cific location. The Stealth To command is also used in conjunction with the WHERE commands.

Regroup: Saying or choosing "Regroup" will order your team to come back to your position. This command is helpful when they become separated from you, or you need backup in a firefight.

Follow: Saying or choosing "Follow" will command your team to follow you. Along with "Hold Position," this command is one of the most commonly used throughout the game.

Hold Position: Saying or choosing "Hold Position" will order your team to stay where they are. This command is extreme-ly useful when extra stealth is required and you don't want to risk the chance of someone seeing your team members.

Bang/Clear: Saying or choosing "Bang/Clear" will command your team to first throw a Flashbang and then clear a room. This command will only become available if you are pointing your cross hairs at a closed door.

Frag/Clear: Saying or choosing "Frag/Clear" will command your team to first throw a deadly Frag grenade and then clear a room. This command will only become available if you are pointing your cross hairs at a closed door.

Clear: Saying or choosing "Clear" will order your team to clear out a room behind your cross hairs. Like the other two Clear commands, this will only become available if you are pointing your cross hairs at a closed door.

Open Door: Saying or choosing "Open Door" will command your team to open a closed door. The Open Door command will only appear if you are pointing your cross hairs over a closed door.

Close Door: Saying or choosing "Close Door" will command your team to close an opened door. The Close Door com-mand will only appear if you are pointing your cross hairs over an open door.

WHERE and HOW:

Frag: Used with "Deploy," saying or choosing "Frag" will order your team to throw a Frag grenade at your cross hairs.

Bang: Used with "Deploy," saying or choosing "Bang" will order your team to throw a Frag grenade at your cross hairs.

Smoke: Used with "Deploy," saying or choosing "Smoke" will order your team to throw a Smoke grenade at your cross hairs.

Satchel: Used with "Deploy," saying or choosing "Satchel" will order your team to place a Satchel charge at your cross hairs.

C-4: Used with "Deploy," saying or choosing "C-4" will order your team to place a C-4 explosive at your cross hairs.

Locations: Depending on your mission, there will be a variety of Nav points you can order your team to head to using the "Run To," "Lead To," "Attack To," and "Stealth To" commands. These locations, which range from "Charlie to Zulu" are dis-played on your TACMAP. You can also order your team to move to your "Cross hairs" as well.

TEAM STATUS:

Maintaining control of your team is crucial for mission success. It is very important to know where they are, what they are doing, and what their current condition is at all times. There is a Team Status menu in the bottom right corner of the screen that gives you all the information you need.

ACTION STATUS:

When there is a change in status of a team member, a description will appear next to the SEAL's name in the bottom right corner of the screen. For example, when you order "Bravo to Run to Whiskey," you will see the information that Jester is "Traveling" to the Nav Point and Spectre is "Following" him. You will also know when they have reached the position, as the Action Status will change from "Traveling" to "Holding".

HEALTH STATUS:

You can also use the Team Status menu to view the current stage of each team member, including yourself. Next to each name in the Team Status menu are small colored squares. The color green indicates that there are no injuries. The color yellow indicates that there are slight injuries. The color orange indicates that there are moderate injuries and combat efficiency is impaired. The color Red indicates there are life-threatening injuries but it is still possible to carry out the mission. The color gray indicates that the SEAL is incapacitated.

HELP MENUS:

During the game, a variety of Help menus will pop up for specific scenarios or instances, pausing the gameplay in the process. These menus are extremely helpful, especially for beginning players, but they can be turned off via the Pause screen.

HEADING INTO A MISSION:

Before heading into each mission, you are given a Mission Briefing, as well as an opportunity to see the current list of Primary Objectives, survey the intelligence HQ has on the area (in the form of a Map), get an Overview and Mission Details, and visit the Armory to manually choose your weapons and trade out the default ones already chosen. We've listed the Overview text for each mission in this guide, as well as the Primary and Secondary Objectives and Maps, but you can check out the Mission Details if you want a little more background information before going in.

13

THE ARMORY:

The Armory screen is accessible before heading in to each mission. You can choose to change weapons for the whole team, each element, or individual SEAL team members, but the default equipment issued to each unit is typically the way to go. Be warned, using an improper weapon (such as a non-silenced rifle) may compromise your mission. To change weapons or equipment, at the Armory screen, press the directional pad or left analog stick up or down to select Fire Team, Able, Bravo, or a specific SEAL and press the ⊗ button. Next, select a LOADOUT Option and press the ⊗ button. This can be the primary weapon, secondary weapon or equipment you want to change. From here, you can cycle through your available options by pressing the directional button or the left analog stick left or right, and can exchange the weapon by selecting the one you want and pressing the ⊗ button.

THE TACMAP SCREEN:

The TACMAP (Tactical Map) screen is where you can view your objectives, see a Tactical Map of the environment, and locate the Mission Path. To access the TACMAP screen, just press the Select button during gameplay.

OBJECTIVES:

During a mission you will be presented with a set of Primary and Secondary objectives. Primary Objectives are mandatory, meaning you must fulfill them in order to have mission success. Secondary Objectives can be passed over, but you will be graded on your performance and you should try to complete every one. We have written this guide with a focus on completing each objective. The objective list will be on the left side of the TACMAP screen and you can view a short movie for each to get more clues and information on how to complete them by highlighting the one you want and pressing the ⊗ button. There is also a check box next to each one and they will be checked off as they are completed. Lastly, you can refer to the objective list underneath the map for each mission in this guide. Some objectives appear mid-way through a level and won't show up in the TACMAP screen until you get to them.

THE TACTICAL MAP:

The Tactical Map is drawn from mission intelligence gathered prior to insertion of the team and is a vital mission tool. The Map can tell you essential information, such as your and your SEAL team positions, major structures, landmarks or geographical features, Navigation Points (operational positions, such as Charlie, Foxtrot, Romeo, etc., that your team must travel to in order to carry out the mission -- they can also be used to direct your team by issuing commands), and the Mission Path. You can zoom in and out of the Map by pressing the right analog stick up and down. You can also move the map around by pressing the left analog stick in any direction.

MEDALS, REWARDS AND RANKS:

Upon completing a mission, you will be given a Mission Statistics screen. On this screen, you will receive a grade for your performance, which is based on Stealth, Accuracy, Teamwork, how many of the Primary and Secondary Objectives you completed and the overall percentage of the mission you completed. To get an A, you will have to use teamwork and use all of your SEAL team members to the best of their abilities.

SOCOM has eight levels of difficulty (as well as a few extra goodies) that can be successively unlocked every time you complete the game. Each time you beat the game, you are promoted in rank. You start off as Ensign, but can go all the way up to Admiral if you're good. Below is the list of ranks and what you are rewarded with each time you complete the game's single player missions in full.

Rank: Ensign
Reward for completing the game = Unlock all terrorist weapons for use in the single player missions (available in the Armory) and a higher difficulty level.

Rank: Lieutenant Jr. Grade
Reward for completing the game = Unlock a level select for the single player levels (so you can choose them separately and in any order) and a higher difficulty level.

Rank: Lieutenant
Reward for completing the game = Unlock the Multiple Grenade Launcher (MGL) and a higher difficulty level.

Rank: Lieutenant Commander
Reward for completing the game = Higher difficulty level.

Rank: Commander
Reward for completing the game = Higher difficulty level.

Rank: Captain
Reward for completing the game = Higher difficulty level.

Rank: Rear Admiral
Reward for completing the game = Higher difficulty level.

Rank: Admiral
Reward for completing the game = Higher difficulty level.

GENERAL TIPS, STRATEGIES, AND OTHER COOL STUFF:

Stealth is the true way to play this game. While there are times when a fierce firefight is required and even recommended, it is much more important that you tackle each mission slowly and carefully, using the environment, shadows, darkness and whatever other means you can think of to be stealthy and silent. Teamwork is also key. Your fellow SEAL team members are a great resource and asset and they should be utilized to the fullest. Make sure to use them for cover, to clear areas, and help you in completing your objectives. This is not a solo effort. Read all of the Help menus that pop up, and watch all of the objective movies in the TACMAP screen, as they will provide you with invaluable information. Lastly, patience is the key to success. Don't react without taking the time to watch and listen. Many times you will come across a group of enemies that will split up if you wait, giving you much better odds at eliminating them without revealing your presence.

While there really aren't any secrets or codes, there are a few things in the game that haven't been documented. One is the ability to make enemies surrender more easily. Using the Headset, you can press the Command (◎) button and scream "Hands in the air! Get Down!" when you enter a room or area with one or two terrorists inside. Doing so will greatly improve the chance that they will drop their weapons and surrender. Another cool secret is ambushing the outhouse on Mission 2 (Operation Ghost Town.) When you come across the outhouse at the end of the mission, you can place your extra C-4 charge on its side and blow it sky high (taking the terrorist inside along with it.) Listen for your SEAL team members to make a hilarious crack when you do it. Lastly, you can kick open closed doors by holding down the Action (✗) button and releasing it when you approach the door. If you time it correctly, you will kick open the door with force instead of opening it slowly by hand.

ALASKA: OPERATION FROSTBITE
MISSION 1: DEATH AT SEA

MISSION OVERVIEW:

"Okay, team. We've got a complicated Recon mission requiring stealth and discretion. We're sure you can handle it, SEALs. We've learned that former Spetznaz operatives have established a new terrorist organization and are using a barge as a vehicle for buying and transporting weapons. They make their trades with a known Black Marketing organization, the Zemy. The two are rendezvousing in international waters off the coast of Alaska. Intercept and eliminate the terrorists, gather as much Intel as possible and scuttle the freighter. Work quietly, men. Stay in the shadows whenever possible."

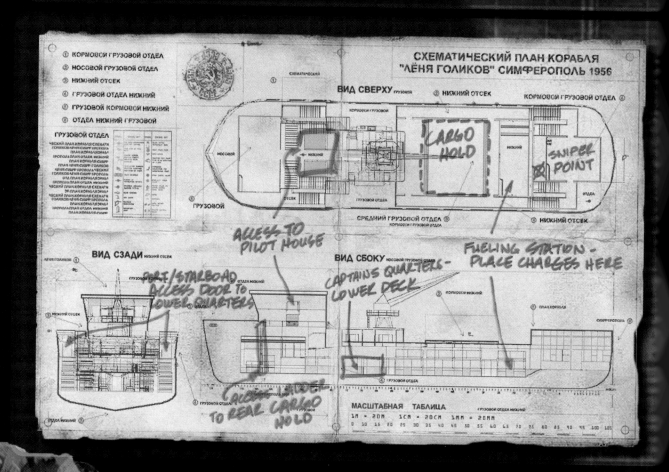

OBJECTIVES

PRIMARY OBJECTIVES

1. SECURE THE BARGE
2. SEVER COMMUNICATIONS
3. COLLECT INTEL
4. SCUTTLE FREIGHTER

SECONDARY OBJECTIVES

1. Dispatch Guard
2. Recon Sentries
3. Reach Freighter
4. Eavesdrop for Intel
5. Plant Charges

BONUS OBJECTIVE

1. Find Iron Manifesto

SECONDARY OBJECTIVE 1: DISPATCH GUARD

Your first objective is to eliminate the two guards patrolling in the immediate area, located straight ahead, just beyond the container at 12:00. Make sure to use the cover of darkness, shadows and large containers to your advantage. You can get close enough to eavesdrop on their conversation by slowly making your way around the containers to your left and over to the stacked crates just behind them.

Order Bravo in a holding position and find a good position to crouch down and wait for the two guards to finish talking. When their conversation comes to an end, one of them will take leave, giving you the perfect opportunity to silently kill the other who remains behind. Wait until you are sure the guard has moved out of sight and then quickly creep up behind the other and silently take him out with either your combat knife or a rifle butt to the head.

SILENT KILL

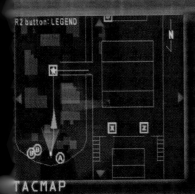

There will be many times where stealth will be required to fulfill a mission objective. You will have to keep from being heard in addition to staying out of sight to keep the enemy from discovering your presence. Whenever possible, it's highly recommended you use a well-placed rifle butt to an enemy's head, or slit his throat with your combat knife. These moves are executed by silently moving right next to the enemy, preferably from behind and in the standing position, and then pressing the Attack ✖ button when the corresponding icon appears on-screen.

PRIMARY OBJECTIVE 2: SECURE THE BARGE

This leaves a total of three guards left on the Barge. The second guard should have only walked a few paces back around the opposite side of the stacked crates. Equip your Nightvision Goggles and peek around the crates. Quickly get a bead on him and take him out with a head shot before he sees you.

NIGHTVISION GOGGLES

Nightvision Goggles are standard issue during nighttime missions and are essential when trying to pinpoint an enemy's location in the dark. You can activate them by pressing forward twice on the D-pad. You can still shoot while they are equipped.

CONTINGENCY PLAN

If things go wrong right off the bat, don't panic. If you're spotted or heard, most likely more guards will come down from the Freighter combat-ready. Stay in a crouched position and try to pick them off as they come down the gangplank. You are going to have to stay alert and be ready for anything, as you'll come to find the enemy is highly unpredictable.

Once the immediate two guards have been eliminated, take a moment to pick up their bodies and move them into the cover of the shadows behind the stacked wooden crates. You can shoot out the sodium lights on the freighter and barge, but doing so will alert any guards still in the area. Hold off for the moment!

BODY DISPOSAL

Dead bodies are a dead giveaway, betraying your presence if they are spotted by an enemy. When stealth is your primary goal, it's best to pick up a fallen foe and move them to an area either hidden from your enemies, or one that is in complete darkness. To pick up a dead body, position yourself either on top of it or right next to it until the "Pick Up Body" icon appears. If there are multiple icons, hold down the Action ✕ button and use the D-pad to cycle through your choices until the proper one is highlighted. Let go of the Action ✕ button when you have chosen the right one. To drop the body, simply press the Action ✕ button once again.

Silently move along the path between the stacked wooden crates and the Barge wall until you come to the end of the second set of crates. There are two more guards stationed off to the northwest, between two shipping containers. Crouch down, using the wooden crates or containers for cover, and patiently wait for their conversation to end. One of the guards complains that he is queasy and takes leave from the other (presumably to find a place to be sick). Wait for him to move out of sight before slowly following him. Stay in the crouched position and keep the stacked wooden crates in between you and him, using them for cover. When you hear him begin to vomit, that's your cue to move in and take him out. You can either rush in and head-butt him with your rifle, or stay back a bit and pick him off with a shot to the head.

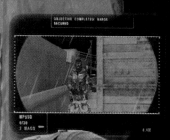

Equip your Nightvision Goggles for the last kill. The remaining guard is patrolling somewhere around the southern-most area of the Barge, which is populated with large metallic shipping containers. He typically can be found between the Barge and the Freighter, behind the stack of wooden crates near the gangplank. He will eventually wind his way through the maze of containers, making it hard for you to locate him. Slowly make your way around, using the shadows and darkness for cover, until you get a bead on him. Listen for Boomer, as he might spot him and give you a reading on the enemy's whereabouts. When he goes down, the Barge should be secured.

LIGHTS OUT

The sodium lights set up around the Barge will also betray you and your team members' presence if you stay out in the open for too long. You can create more darkness, and places to hide, by shooting them out with your weapon. Make sure that there are no guards in the immediate area when you do so, as the noise might alert them to your presence.

SECONDARY OBJECTIVE 2: RECON SENTRIES

There are two snipers placed in key locations on the north and south ends of the Freighter. If they spot you, your silent insertion will be blown. Make your way back to the center of the Barge, find a secure spot next to a stack of wooden crates or a shipping container and equip your Nightvision Goggles.

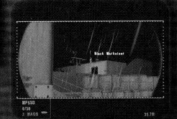

The first sniper is off to the right, on the north side of the Freighter. He is patrolling up on the elevated deck. You will get a confirmation when he is in your sights. Keep your HK5SD equipped and silently take him out when you have a clean shot. Stay on him with your cross hairs and make sure he doesn't get back up. It's possible you might alert a secondary guard (a Black Marketeer), patrolling the area below the upper deck. If so, he will run up the stairs to investigate. Take a few extra seconds and watch to see if he makes a move. If so, you will need to quickly take him out as well.

The second sniper is off to the left, on the opposite, south side of the Freighter. He is also patrolling up on an elevated area, right next to the Pilot House. Again, get a bead on him with your HK5SD rifle and silently take him out with a clean shot or two.

SECONDARY OBJECTIVE 3: REACH FREIGHTER

Your way to the Freighter should almost be clear. Before heading up the gangplank and onto the Freighter, make sure there are no other patrolling guards on its deck. There should be a Black Marketer (the one that was below where you shot the first sniper) on the north side of the ship. To get a clean shot, climb up on a stack of wooden crates (the set back and to the right of the gangplank is best) and take him out silently with your HK5SD.

CLIMBING

It's possible (and very necessary) to climb up onto objects in order to get a better vantage point for targeting, or pull yourself up onto a higher ledge, object or ladder. When you need to climb onto an object, position yourself right next to it. If you can climb it, a "Climb" icon will appear. Press the Action button to execute the command.

Now that your path is relatively clear, get into the prone position and crawl up the gangplank, taking a left toward the cover of the stacked crates when you reach the top.

STAND, CROUCH AND PRONE

There are three positions you can take, each necessary to achieve your objectives. When standing, you are most vulnerable and can easily be seen by the enemy, but you can quickly run and maneuver. In the standing position, your aiming is the least accurate. Crouching allows you to slowly walk in a crouched position, making it harder to be seen. It also gives you the ability to duck down and take cover behind objects. This position is quite useful and should be used in most situations. When crouched, your aim is more accurate than when standing. The Prone position allows you to get down on your belly and crawl. Crawling is useful when you want to avoid the enemy's line of sight or hide in foliage. In the Prone position, your aim is the most accurate.

TACMAP

SECONDARY OBJECTIVE 4: EAVESDROP FOR INTEL

When you get to the stacked crates, you will hear the conversation between the Captain of the Freighter and the Iron Leader. When their brief conversation ends, stay either prone or crouched and tuck yourself in close next to the stacked wooden crates. The Iron Leader will head for the shelter of one of the small rooms on deck.

Watch and wait for him to head inside, then order Bravo to follow. They will slowly make their way onto the Freighter.

When your team has regrouped, carefully take out the Iron Leader. The door to the room should be open and there is a good chance he will be waiting for you. Hug the right wall and peek into the doorway, then quickly take him out.

There is another terrorist inside the second room to the right. If he hasn't already come out to investigate, quickly open the door and eliminate him as well.

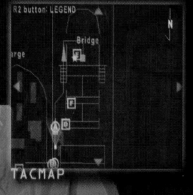

Before moving on to your next objective, it's a good idea to clear the deck on any terrorists and Black Marketers that might be patrolling the area. There should be at least one or two in the general vicinity, including the captain of the Freighter. Slowly make your way around the perimeter, eliminating any enemies you find.

PRIMARY OBJECTIVE 2: SEVER COMMUNICATIONS

When the coast is generally clear, head up the south stairs toward the Pilot House. There is another stairwell leading up to the Pilot House here. If you start to make your way up the second set, you will find that there are two guards protecting the Pilot House. Quickly back down the stairs and use the cover of the wall to the right of the doorway to listen in on their conversation. If you patiently wait for a few seconds, one of the guards may leave his post to go on patrol, leaving just one remaining in the Pilot House. If he does, wait for the other to disappear down the opposite stairwell and then slowly make your way up the stairs. If he doesn't leave, slowly walk up the stairs to the doorway, but don't let them see you.

If you peek into the Pilot House, you can watch the guard(s) without being detected. Wait until you have a clean shot and quickly take them out. Use the element of surprise to your advantage, and make sure they don't get to the Comm Unit before you eliminate them.

The Communications Unit is inside the Pilot House to your right, sitting atop the counter next to some maps and charts. You can either shoot it or move your cursor over it and press your Action ⊗ button when the "Comm Unit" icon appears on screen. Either way, you will have severed the terrorists' communications and completed your objective.

PRIMARY OBJECTIVE 3: COLLECT INTEL

Head down the opposite stairwell and out onto the deck. If the guard went on his patrol from the Pilot House, he should be out here, and has, most likely, seen the carnage you left behind. Be ready for him and take him out.

It's time to head down into the lower-half of the Freighter. Take the stairwell leading down to your left. For the most part, the inside of the Freighter is comprised of cramped hallways and corridors. Stay alert, and be ready for enemies hiding around blind corners. You'll most likely encounter the first one at the bottom of the stairs just around the corner. Make use of the walls here, peeking around corners and doorways to keep from being seen. It's much easier to take out an enemy who doesn't know you're there. You can also shoot out the lights along the walls, making it harder for the terrorists to spot you.

Take an immediate left and go down the second set of stairs. You will find yourselves at an intersection. If you're lucky, the patrolling guard to the right will be taking a smoke. You should be able to catch him unaware and deliver a solid head-butt with your rifle before he even knows what hit him.

Take a left at the intersection. The Ledger (Shipping Manifest) is located in the room to the right (behind the closed door). There are more than likely two guards patrolling down here — one at the end of the hallway and another behind one of the two closed doors. Collect the Ledger when you have taken them out.

BONUS OBJECTIVE: FIND IRON MANIFESTO

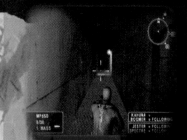

Before scuttling the Freighter, there is the matter of the Iron Manifesto. This bonus item has been casually left up on a stack of wooden crates in the north cargo hold. Follow the main corridor out into the next intersection (with the two industrial fans), and then either take a left or right and head down into the next corridor toward the red-lit doorway. There are two doorways down here. The red-lit one connects with the other, which leads into the north cargo hold. Before entering the cargo hold, take a moment to peek into the red-lit corridor and eliminate the two enemies standing guard. Head into the cargo hold and climb up onto the large concentration of wooden crates, which are stacked in the east (back left) corner. You'll find the Iron Manifesto sitting atop the second level of crates — yours for the taking.

TACMAP

SECONDARY OBJECTIVE 5: PLANT CHARGES

In order to scuttle the Freighter, you need to plant two Satchel Charges in two key locations in this red-lit corridor. If you walk up to the set of panels at either end of the corridor, you will be given the option to do so via a "Place Satchel" icon. Press the Action ✗ button to plant the first one. Since you only have one Satchel Charge in your inventory, you will need to command one of your other SEAL team members to place the second.

Point your cross hairs at the second set of panels and order either Able or Bravo to Deploy Satchel Charge.

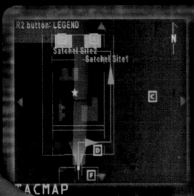

TACMAP

PRIMARY OBJECTIVE 4: SCUTTLE FREIGHTER

Depending on who you commanded, one of your team members will place the final Satchel Charge, completing the final remaining mission objective. Well done SEALs!

ALASKA: OPERATION FROSTBITE
MISSION 2: GHOST TOWN

MISSION OVERVIEW:

"Good work on that barge, team. Luckily, this next mission won't be such a wet one. As we suspected, the terrorists have established a strong base in Alaska. We need you to gather information on their activities, detain the terrorist Kola Petranko for questioning and send a clear message to these trespassers. The United States does not sanction terrorist activities on her soil, and while Alaska may be cold, it is still part of the U.S. Systematically destroy the terrorist's weapon and supply caches. Good luck, team."

OBJECTIVES

PRIMARY OBJECTIVES
1. OBTAIN INTEL
2. SECURE COMPOUND
3. DESTROY WEAPONS
4. EXTRACT CAPTIVE

SECONDARY OBJECTIVES
1. Bravo To Charlie
2. Neutralize Sentry
3. Insert Into Mission
4. Bravo Cover Dredge
5. Secure Lodge
6. Secure Cabin
7. Secure Mining House
8. Secure "Pincushion"

TACMAP

SECONDARY OBJECTIVE 1: BRAVO TO CHARLIE

In order to achieve a clean insertion, you have to keep from being seen by the enemy. You only have a few precious seconds before you'll be spotted by a sentry who is making his rounds.

Order Bravo to Run To nav point Charlie, which is just on the other side of the abandoned cabin. Not only will they be able to take cover and keep from being spotted, but they will also be able to provide you with support in case you get into a hostile situation.

TACMAP

SECONDARY OBJECTIVE 2: NEUTRALIZE SENTRY

While Bravo heads off for Charlie, you and Boomer need to find some cover of your own. Make your way to the inside of the broken down cabin and take cover. When you are inside, assume the prone position and look through your M4 A1 SD Rifle's scope.

SNIPING AND THE ADRENALINE FACTOR

Some weapons are equipped with scopes that offer varying levels of magnification, allowing you to zoom in and out with the Directional button. When equipped, you can press forward on the Directional button once, in order to get into the first-person perspective, and then press a second time to look through your rifle's scope. Some scopes have multiple levels of zoom. To zoom in even closer, press the Directional button forward once more. You can zoom back out by pressing down on the Directional button as well.

When aiming with your scope, you will have to take into account the adrenaline coursing through your veins. In these tense situations your heart will beat faster than normal and you might have a harder time keeping your sights trained on your target. When aiming your scope at an enemy, make slow, precise movements and give yourself a moment to calm down before adjusting your aim.

If you position yourself just inside the cabin, facing west, you should be able to see an outcropping of trees off in the distance and still be covered by a portion of the cabin wall. A lone sentry will be coming from this way in just a moment. Order Bravo to Fire At Will, giving them the opportunity to take out any hostiles while you keep your scope focused on this area. The sentry will eventually show himself. Be patient and wait for him to get close enough to get a clean shot off.

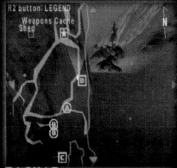

R2 button: LEGEND
Weapons Cache
Shed

TACMAP

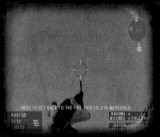

SECONDARY OBJECTIVE 3: INSERT INTO MISSION

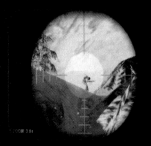

Head out north. You should see a small ridge dead ahead. Leave Bravo at their holding point for the moment and make your way to it and then climb up to the area above. Off to the right, there is a higher ridge with a sentry patrolling its perimeter. There's a good chance Bravo took him out from their vantage point. Be patient, hug the mountain wall and wait to see if he comes into view (if he's still alive, you should be able to hear him complaining about the cold). When you have a clean shot, take it.

Order Bravo to Follow and climb up the ridge to the next elevation. Use the mountain wall to your left as a guide (and for cover) and slowly make your way north. Whenever you get to a blind corner, be sure to stop in the crouched position and peek out to survey the area. There is at least one more sentry making his rounds in the general vicinity. Take him out before he spots you.

FOOTPRINTS

The snowy Alaskan terrain can be used to your advantage. You'll notice that you leave footprints in the snow. This goes the same for the enemy. If you stay aware of your surroundings, you might be able to tell if a guard has been in the vicinity and which way he was heading.

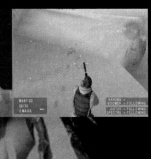

If you continue to follow the left side of the mountain wall, you will eventually come to an opening. Take a left and follow the opening out, which leads to a valley below; home to a series of abandoned cabins and now the ramshackle base of the enemy. Objective accomplished.

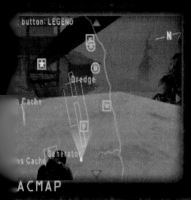

ACMAP

SECONDARY OBJECTIVE 4: BRAVO COVER DREDGE

The Intel you're looking for is a Laptop computer. Intelligence places it in the Dredge, which is off to the northwest. You are going to have to eliminate some of the opposition on your way over there. To start, use your elevated position on the mountainside to your advantage. Position yourself at the edge of the ridge, get into the prone position, and either pull out your Binoculars or use your sniper scope to survey the surroundings below.

BINOCULARS

When you have a primary weapon equipped that is not furnished with a scope (assault rifle, machine gun, etc.), or a secondary weapon (pistol), you can activate your Binoculars by pressing up on the Directional button. To deactivate them, press down on the Directional button.

You should be able to spot one of the terrorists at 2:00. Using your vantage point and your M4A1 SD rifle, zoom in and pick him off.
There will most likely be a few more guards patrolling the area below. There should be another, farther off in the distance, somewhere around 10:00 to 11:00. Take him out, and any others, only if you can get clean shots off. There's no need to alert the enemy to your presence otherwise.

There may be a sniper in a prone position stationed off to the northeast. He will most likely be laying down on the ground, making it harder to spot him. Use your scope to locate and eliminate him.

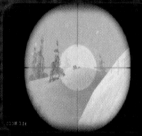

Follow the ridge down to the north but don't head out into the valley. You are going to want to keep the buildings to your left. When you get to the bottom, head into the gap between the two hills on your right and go back up. If you get turned around, you can always stop and look at your Tactical Map (TACMAP) by pressing the Select button.

27

THE TACMAP

The Tactical Map (TACMAP) is provided to give you and your team a quick look at your surroundings. To access the TACMAP, press the Select button, which pauses the game and pulls up the map and objectives screen. You can use the in-game TACMAP to get your bearings, find the mission path, see the location of your nav points, locate your fellow SEAL team members, and get a bead on the general location of each of your mission objectives. We have also provided a shot of the TACMAP next to each objective in the guide, giving you a quick reference of where you need to be heading and the best path to get you there with the least amount of resistance.

When you get up on the mountainside, start heading west. Keep up and away from the cabins below and head north/northwest until you come down into the valley on the other side of the small fence. Off to the left is a broken down building holding a running Generator and off in the distance is the Dredge.

 Quickly go into the building and switch off the Generator by approaching it and pressing the Action (✖) button, then head back over to the area on the other side of the fence.

The area surrounding the Dredge is guarded heavily, and you will need to use Bravo as cover when you go in. To do so, you will have to send them to Nav Point Zulu by way of Whiskey and X-Ray. Stay put in the general area and order Bravo to Run To Whiskey. When they get to Whiskey order them to Run To X-Ray. Finally, when they have arrived at X-Ray, order Bravo to Run to Zulu. While you are waiting for Bravo to get to Zulu, you might encounter a lone enemy sentry. Stay crouched or in the prone position and keep an eye out, especially around the 11:00 position. The objective will be complete when Bravo arrives at Zulu.

ACTION STATUS

When there is a change in status of a team member, a description will appear next to the man's name in the bottom right corner of the screen. For example, when you order Bravo to Run to Whiskey, you will see the information that Jester is "Traveling" to the Nav Point and Spectre is "Following" him. You will also know when they have reached the position, as the Action Status will change from "Traveling" to "Holding".

PRIMARY OBJECTIVE 1: OBTAIN INTEL

MAP

The Dredge is heavily guarded and, from the intelligence gathered, it's also wired with motion sensor alarms. Since you've shut down the Generator, the alarms should be out of commission. Even if you disconnect it, the alarm may still be active, so be prepared for the worst. If the alarm is tripped, you'll alert the enemy to your presence, but you can at least even the odds by stealthfully picking off the enemies you can find before going in. Once Bravo has reached Zulu, slowly make your way toward the Dredge. When you get close enough to have a good view of its interior, get into the prone position, take a look through your scope and try to locate any guards patrolling inside. There are at least two. Pick them off as quickly and cleanly as possible. If given the opportunity, they will activate the alarm

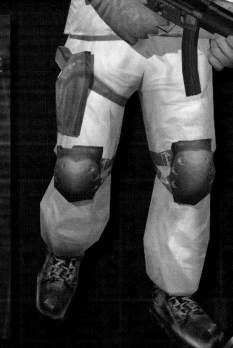

If the alarm is activated, you'll only have three minutes to locate the Intel. You're looking for a Laptop which contains critical data on the Iron Brotherhood's operations. If the enemy knows you're here, they will start taking the steps to erase the data before you can get to it.

SETTING YOUR WEAPON'S FIRE MODE

Many assault weapons have multiple firing modes, allowing you to change the rate of fire from single shot to burst. Depending on the weapon you are carrying, you can set it up to a three shot burst. To switch firing modes, press down on the L3 button (the left analog stick). The Bullet icon on the Weap-on in Hand display in the left corner of the screen will change from one to three (burst) or more (for fully automatic weapons, such as the M4A1 SD).

Set your weapon's fire mode to burst and head into the opening on the left side of the Dredge. If you've tripped the alarm, don't waste any precious seconds exploring the bottom floor — you need to get upstairs and find the Laptop fast.

Take the stairs up to the second level, making sure to quickly eliminate any guards as you do. There is no way around the motion sensors above each staircase. If the Generator has been reactivated, you will trip the alarm. Since time is of the essence, you won't have the luxury of stealth. Come at the enemy hard and fast before they have a chance to return fire.

There is a second set of stairs along the left side of the Dredge leading to the third floor and there should be at least two to more guards located up there. If you've tripped the alarm, one of them will most likely be on his way to engage you and the other will try and make quick work of the sensitive data in the Laptop before you can stop him. Take them out as fast as possible. Every second counts.

If you have tripped the alarm, you can switch it off when it is safe to do so. The switch is set against the wall to the left of the desk. To do so, walk up to it and press the Action (✖) button when the "Flip Switch" icon appears. This should, for the moment, stop any more guards from coming that aren't already on their way.

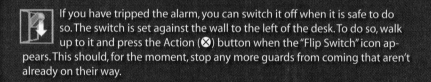

If your cover is blown, you will have to be very careful if you want to get out of the Dredge alive. The Laptop is just around the corner from the stairs sitting on a desk. Quickly walk up to it and press the Action (✖) button when the "Take Laptop" icon appears. There are multiple exits out of the Dredge, including a few doors that lead onto the roof, but the best route out is the same way you came in. As soon as you have grabbed the Laptop, take the stairs back down to the second floor.

If you tripped the alarm, you should have enough time to prepare for the enemies heading your way. Be on the lookout for any sentries coming in from the back-left entrance on the bottom floor. It's also possible Bravo will take care of them before they ever even make it inside the Dredge.

PRIMARY OBJECTIVE 2: SECURE COMPOUND

TACMAP

It's time to secure the entire compound, find "Pincushion," and get to the Extraction Point. To do so, you will have to go from building to building, clearing each one as you go. You won't actually complete this objective until all of the buildings in the compound have been secured. Order Bravo to Follow and prepare to head out.

SECONDARY OBJECTIVE 5: SECURE LODGE

TACMAP

The first building on your route is the Lodge. Refer to the path on your TACMAP and then head out in an easterly direction. The broken down building with the Generator inside is on the way to the Lodge. Go there first. As you approach, you will find that there are more guards on snowmobiles coming your way. Take cover and get ready for another fire fight. The enemy will be approaching from the southwest, coming over the small hill on the left of the Dredge.

It's possible you alerted the enemy to your presence, so surprise might not be an option. Use stealth and reconnaissance from a distance to see if you can spot any guards outside the Lodge. There are a total of three terrorists guarding the lodge. If they are not outside, be very careful, and approach the Lodge from the side, using its wall for cover. There is only one door into the Lodge and three terrorists will come pouring out of it if they hear you. Stay on the side of the Lodge, use the wall for cover and pick them off if they come out.

SILENT MOVEMENT

Crouch-walking and crawling is useful for more than just staying out of the enemy's line of vision. When slowly moving in these positions, the enemy will also be less likely be able to hear your approach. You can use this to your advantage when the element of surprise is a necessity.

If you were quiet enough, you can use Able or Bravo to Clear the Lodge. To do so, aim your cross hairs at the closed door and order either Bravo or Able to Bang/Clear or Frag/Clear. Your SEAL team member will throw a Grenade inside the building to harm or disorient the enemy, then go in and clean up the leftovers.

CLEARING BUILDINGS

In many instances, it's beneficial to order one of your other SEAL team members to clear an area or building. In order to do so, the door to the building must be closed. When clearing a building or area, aim your cross hairs at the closed door and then order Bravo or Able to either Bang/Clear or Frag/Clear. The command Bang/Clear will order your team members to first throw in a Flash Grenade, and then enter the building, temporarily stunning and disorienting the enemy. The command Frag/Clear will order your SEAL team members to first throw a Grenade into the building, harming or killing the enemy first, before entering and clearing.

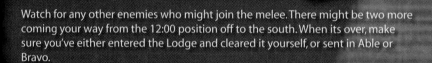

Watch for any other enemies who might join the melee. There might be two more coming your way from the 12:00 position off to the south. When its over, make sure you've either entered the Lodge and cleared it yourself, or sent in Able or Bravo.

PRIMARY OBJECTIVE 3: DESTROY WEAPONS

TACMAP

The Iron Brotherhood is storing their weapons in stacked crates throughout the area. You are going to have to destroy them by deploying a C-4 charge on each one. There are a total of three sets of Weapon Caches; one next to the Lodge, one in front of a Shed off to the north, and the last next to the Bosler House. You won't be able to complete this objective until they are all destroyed.

 The first Weapons Cache is just to the left of the front door of the Lodge. Make sure your SEAL team members are far away from the general vicinity of the Cache and Order Bravo to Hold Position. While not designed for an anti-personnel role, C-4 can be fatal to anyone caught within the radius of its blast, including your own team members.

SELECTING AND USING YOUR WEAPONS CACHE

You and your SEAL team members can carry or hold a finite amount of weapons and items. To access your Weapons Cache, press the `R2` button. This brings up a menu in the left side of the screen, allowing you to cycle through your inventory with the Directional button by pressing up or down. To equip the one you want, highlight it and press the `R2` button again or the Action (✖) button. That item will appear in the Weapon in Hand display in the bottom-left corner of the screen.

Select the C-4 from your inventory, and then position yourself in front of the Weapons Cache. Press the `R1` button to attach the C-4 to the crates and then make sure you run out of range of the blast. You have ten seconds to clear the blast.

Leave Bravo in a holding position and then continue heading south toward the Shed and the second Weapons Cache. Make sure to re-equip your rifle or pistol as you head out. Also be on the look out for any hostiles that might have heard the explosion and are coming to investigate. The second Weapons Cache should be dead ahead. Select the C-4 again and quickly attach it to the stacked crates. Clear the blast radius and that's two down, one to go.

TACMAP

SECONDARY OBJECTIVE 6: SECURE CABIN

Order Bravo to Follow and slowly make your way around the back side of the Shed (the front side faces the mountain region where you inserted into the area). There is a window in back that should give you a clear view of the enemy inside, who is most likely guarding the front door. Get a bead on him and take him out, through the window, with a clean head shot.

The next building, the Cabin, is just off to the southwest. There are three to four guards stationed in or around the Cabin and they may or may not be alerted to your presence (you might also have killed one or two earlier, when you were sniping from the ridge). With all of the noise you've been making, it's probably a good bet they know you're coming. If the door to the Cabin is open, they are most likely patrolling the area outside. Use precaution and secure the perimeter before closing in on the Cabin. When the area is clear, enter the Cabin to secure it.

If the Cabin door is closed, point your cross hairs at the door and order Able to either Frag / Clear or Bang / Clear. Boomer will throw open the door, toss a Grenade inside and then head in for clean up and secure the Cabin. If you are low on ammunition at this point, it might be a good idea to grab a fallen enemy's weapon and swap it with your M4A1 SD. Be sure to also look for any dropped Magazine Clips while you're at it.

EXCHANGING WEAPONS

You can swap out both your Primary and Secondary weapons with a fallen foe's weapons at any time. While most of the time, you should stick with what you brought into the mission, there will be instances when you are running low or out of ammunition and need another weapon to continue on. To trade weapons, position yourself over the left behind weapon on the ground. When "Take Weapon" icon appears, press the Action (❌) button to drop yours and pick it up.

TACMAP

SECONDARY OBJECTIVE 7: SECURE MINING HOUSE

The next and last building to secure is the Bosler House, a large two room building off to the north. According to intelligence, this is the building where Kola Petrenko, a.k.a. "Pincushion" is located.

Drop down onto the frozen riverbed to the right of the Cabin you just cleared. The riverbed will take you northeast, which is toward the general direction of the House. Make sure you are on the lookout for any enemies down here. There's an outhouse at the base of the riverbed, and there's good chance you might be able to catch one of the terrorists, quite literally, with his pants down. Crouch-walk up to the outhouse and use surprise to your advantage.

When you've eliminated any and all guards in the immediate area, order Bravo to Hold Position and equip your C-4. The last Weapons Cache is right in front of the House. Since you will be securing Pincushion and extracting him from the area, it's better to detonate the crates beforehand, as to not accidently harm him in the explosion. With the last Weapons Cache detonated, your third Primary Objective is now accomplished.

Pincushion is inside, but you should first secure the House's perimeter before restraining him. Instead of heading in through the front door, cautiously move around the front of the building toward the east end (where the snowmobiles are located.) You should find a guard waiting for you on the other side of the dilapidated wall. Eliminating him and entering through the back door should secure the building.

TACMAP

SECONDARY OBJECTIVE 8: SECURE PINCUSHION

Pincushion is in the main room of the House, in front of the fireplace. The moment he sees you, he will drop his weapon and put his hands up, letting you know he is giving himself up. He can be Restrained by approaching him and pressing the Action (✗) button when the "Restrain" icon appears.

RESTRAINING ENEMIES

Sometimes it's necessary to Restrain an enemy or hostage instead of killing them. If an enemy surrenders to you (by putting their weapon down and hands up), you can then Restrain them, rendering them harmless in the process. Oftentimes, a hostile enemy will surrender if he is outnumbered, injured, or lesser-skilled. When an enemy surrenders, approach him and then press the Action (✗) button when the "Restrain" icon appears.

TACMAP

PRIMARY OBJECTIVE 4: EXTRACT CAPTIVE

Now that Pincushion is under your control, he must be extracted from the area alive and in one piece. Order him to Follow by positioning your cross hairs over him and pressing the Action (✗) button when the "Follow" icon appears, and slowly make your way out of the House with him in tow.

ESCORTING

To order an Escortee to follow you, just place the cross hairs over him. When the "Follow" icon appears, press the Action (✗) button to command him to follow. If you want the Escortee to hold his position, place the cross hairs over him once again, until the "Hold Position" icon appears, and press the Action (✗) button. An Escortee will be represented by an "H" inside a circle on your radar. It is a good idea to keep Escortees in your sights at all times. Unarmed and restrained, they are sitting ducks to enemy fire.

Head back down into the riverbed and make your way southeast toward the Extract Zone (which is labeled on your TACMAP and will also show up on your radar as an "X" when you get in its general vicinity.) Don't get too far ahead of Pincushion — even though he is restrained, it's possible he can fall behind or become victim to enemy fire.
When you reach the Extract Zone, your rendezvous helicopter will come in and remove you, Pincushion and your teammates from the area. Another successful mission accomplished!

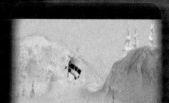

MISSION 3: OIL PLATFORM TAKEDOWN

MISSION OVERVIEW:

"Nice work in Alaska, although destroying the Brotherhood's base hasn't ended their threats. They have taken control of an oil platform in the Alaskan Beaufort Sea. Most of the oil workers on the platform have been killed, but we know some are held captive. The Brotherhood is also threatening to destroy the platform, which would result in a disastrous oil spill. Eliminate all threats, defuse all bombs, and protect the hostages. It's time to teach the Brotherhood their final lesson."

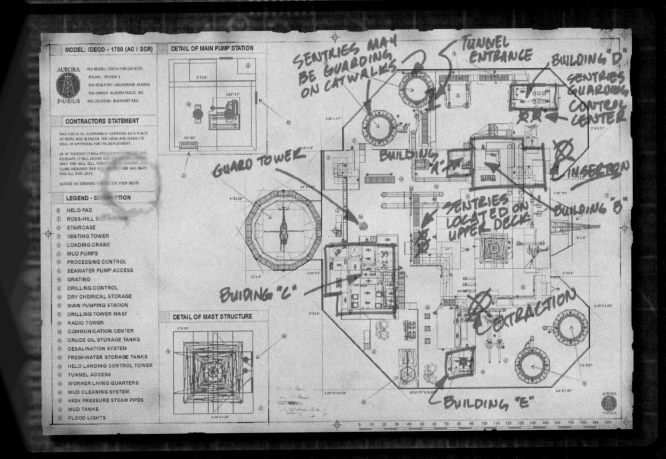

OBJECTIVES

PRIMARY OBJECTIVES

1. DEFUSE THE BOMBS
2. RESCUE THE HOSTAGES
3. SECURE OIL PLATFORM

SECONDARY OBJECTIVES

1. Neutralize Sentries
2. Secure Building D
3. Identify Snipers
4. Neutralize Snipers
5. Clean Insertion
6. Secure Building A
7. Secure Building B
8. Defuse Bomb 1
9. Defuse Bomb 2
10. Defuse Bomb 3
11. Secure Building E
12. Locate Oil Workers
13. Restrain Workers
14. Secure Building C
15. Secure Helipad

TACMAP

PRIMARY OBJECTIVE 1: DEFUSE THE BOMBS

There are a total of three Bombs placed in strategic areas across the Oil Platform. If the Iron Brotherhood leader thinks the Platform is being infiltrated, he won't hesitate to detonate them, leaving you with only four short minutes to locate and defuse each one. Unfortunately, if you are seen or eliminate a sentry who is in communication with the leader, your chances of success will lessen greatly. This objective will not be completed until much later on in the mission.

TACMAP

SECONDARY OBJECTIVE 1: NEUTRALIZE SENTRIES

In order to find the Bombs, you are going to have to silently eliminate any opposition along the way.

There are two sentries stationed in front of the two large metallic crates to your right. Since your insertion point is covered in darkness, you should be able to use the shadows for cover. Slowly make your way around the back side of the crate to your right and peek between them. Wait until at least one of them has his back turned before firing. When you are confident that you can get clean shots off, take them both out quickly and quietly. If you are spotted before you can kill them, you will have failed your Clean Insertion Objective.

If you aren't confident that you can eliminate them both together, you can opt to wait for them to separate and head out on their patrol routes. The sentry on the left will head off to the east, pause, and then return, while the other will enter the building on the right (Building D). This will give you a bit of breathing room, as well as easier kills.

SPECTRUM REPORTING IN

The Iron Brotherhood leader (code-named Spectrum) is in constant communication with many of the sentries patrolling the Platform's perimeter and buildings via radio. There are a total of five sentries carrying radios (code-named Red, Yellow, Green, Blue and Black.) He will check in with them periodically and, if one of them does not make their report, he will become agitated and start the detonation process. If and when he does, you will have a total of four minutes to find and disarm the remaining bombs.

SECONDARY OBJECTIVE 2: SECURE BUILDING D

TACMAP

Building D is the building just off to your right. The main room of the building is empty, although it houses a tunnel underneath that runs along the east side of the Platform. The tunnel has a few guards patrolling its length. It's not necessary to go down there, possibly alerting them to your presence in the process. You can clear Building D by just going through the door and walking inside. As soon as it's cleared, head back out the door you came in.

SECONDARY OBJECTIVE 3: IDENTIFY SNIPERS

TACMAP

Back outside, leave Bravo in a holding position and shoot out the surrounding sodium lights in the immediate area (the large light above the two exhaust fans on the left, and the two lights above the door to Building D.)
Slowly head toward the ramp to the east while hugging the right wall of Building D for cover.

Green is patrolling the ground area between nav points Charlie to Echo. If you are spotted by him, or any of the snipers positioned above you, your Clean Insertion will be blown. Stop at the corner of the wall and make sure Spectrum has finished his first round of checking in. You also don't want to kill Green just yet. Since he has a radio, it's best to leave him be until after you have identified and eliminated the snipers, giving you that much more time to locate and defuse the Bombs.

To your right, just beyond the wall of Building D are a set of large metallic crates. There are three stacked on top of one another, creating a small tunnel between the bottom two and providing a perfect space for cover. Make sure there are no sentries within sight and quickly duck into the space.

Assume the Prone position and crawl up to the opposite end of the tunnel. When you get there, make sure your body is not exposed to the outside area and equip your Binoculars. There are a total of two snipers standing guard stationed above.

The first is straight ahead, atop the oil tower directly to the east.

The second is atop a catwalk diagonally left of you to the north.

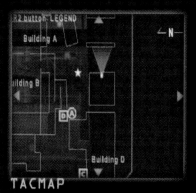

TACMAP

SECONDARY OBJECTIVE 4: NEUTRALIZE SNIPERS

If you chose to stick with the default weapons before entering the mission, you don't have a scope. If you miss your shot and alert the snipers to your presence, your cover will be blown. It's imperative you make sure you have a clean shot before you take it. Take your time and aim for the head of each sniper, taking multiple shots if necessary to insure they are down for the count.

Start with the sniper on the left. Try to stay relatively inside of the tunnel and peek out. When you are sure you have a clean shot, take him down. The second sniper patrolling the oil tower might be a tougher shot. If you are not close enough, he will be out of your rifle's range. Make sure your cross hairs are red before taking the shot.

CROSS HAIRS AND TARGETING

If you haven't noticed by now, your cross hairs will change color from yellow to red when you have an enemy in their sights. The color yellow indicates that you don't have an enemy targeted, or that you can't shoot the enemy from your vantage point. Sometimes he might be out of targeting range and, even though your cross hairs are directly over your target, he is too far away to be struck. Red cross hairs indicate that the enemy is targeted and you will be able to hit them. If you have Assisted Aiming turned on (accessible via the pause screen), you will see a second, red-colored square targeting reticle appear over your targeted enemy. As long as the reticle stays on your targeted enemy, your weapon will be "locked on" to him, guaranteeing a direct hit to the body. Lastly, if there is an obstacle or obstruction in your path, such as a fence railing, tree, wall, etc, you will get a red-colored circle with a line through it, indicating that the targeted enemy can't be hit.

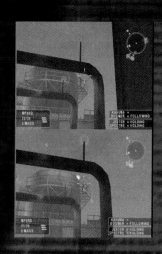

TACMAP

SECONDARY OBJECTIVE 5: CLEAN INSERTION

You should have achieved a clean insertion after neutralizing the two snipers but, before moving on, you still have to deal with Green, who is patrolling the area. Cautiously move out of your hiding space and locate him, then take him out.

Since he is now unable to report in, you are on a short time table to find the bombs and disarm them before they are detonated. You should have a few minutes before the next check in. Use them wisely.

TACMAP

SECONDARY OBJECTIVE 6: SECURE BUILDING A

Order Bravo to Follow, then make your way to Building A (it is directly north — just to the right of Building B.) Be on the lookout for any sentries patrolling the peripheral areas, taking them out in the process. Enter and Clear it yourself. There is a lone guard inside, Yellow, who is not expecting company. When he goes down, Building A will be officially cleared.

DETONATION PROCESS ACTIVATED

By now, Spectrum may be aware of your presence, and may have started the detonation process. The bombs are on a four minute timer, giving you little time to find and disarm them before they blow. Keep an eye on the count down timer on the right side of your screen. If it gets down to zero before you've found and disarmed them all, the whole Platform is going to be obliterated, killing you and your SEAL team mates in the process.

TACMAP

SECONDARY OBJECTIVE 7: SECURE BUILDING B

Building B is next to Building A, just to the left of it. You can gain entrance to Building B by heading up and around the ramp, then taking a right when you get up to the catwalk. Satellite intelligence puts two terrorists inside the Building, making it a much riskier proposition for a lone SEAL to Clear and Secure. Shoot out the lights above the doorway first, giving Bravo team extra cover, and then order Bravo to Frag/Clear the building. All you have to do is wait for them to take care of business before going in and lending support.

TACMAP

SECONDARY OBJECTIVE 8: DEFUSE BOMB 1

That beeping you're hearing is one of the bombs, which is very close by. Make your way through the connecting door inside Building B, which will lead you out onto the upper platform above Building A. The bomb is just to the left of the doorway outside, affixed to one of the Platform's very combustible oil-filled pipelines.

Since time is of the essence, order Able to Defuse the Bomb, then leave him to take care of business while you seek out the next bomb.

DEFUSING BOMBS

You can either order a SEAL team member to defuse a Bomb or you can disarm it yourself. To Defuse a Bomb by yourself, either Crouch down or point your cross hairs over the Bomb and then press the Action (✗) button when the "Defuse Bomb" icon appears. If Spectrum has started the count down process, you probably don't have the luxury of time to single-handedly defuse them all. To order a SEAL team member to defuse a Bomb, point your cross hairs over the Bomb and then order either Bravo or Able to Defuse Bomb. Either way, it will take approximately 25 seconds from start to finish to completely defuse one.

TACMAP

SECONDARY OBJECTIVE 9: DEFUSE BOMB 2

The second Bomb is down the ramp to your right. It is located on the left side, toward the east end of the elevated platform. This one is affixed to a pipe that is connected to one of the oil towers. Before taking on the job of defusing the Bomb, you can utilize your team members to provide some back up support.

There is a ramp behind the oil tower which leads down to a tunnel. If you were to start defusing the Bomb, it's very possible you could be sabotaged by a terrorist coming from this area. Since Bravo is by your side, you can use them to cover the area and give you a little breathing room. To do so, make sure Bravo is in the immediate vicinity, head down the ramp a bit and then point your cross hairs over the door leading to the tunnel. Order Bravo to Cover Area. They will train their weapons in the general vicinity of the doorway, allowing you to go back up and defuse the Bomb. Don't be alarmed if you hear them go into action, they will have the element of surprise on their side and easily take out all and any hostiles that happen to come through the doorway.

COVERING TARGETS

Oftentimes, it is advantageous to have your Bravo SEAL team members provide cover support while you perform a separate task. Having them do so will give you much needed protection, allowing you to concentrate on the matter at hand while they take the heat. To do so, point your cross hairs at the target or area you want covered and then order Bravo to Cover Area.

TACMAP

SECONDARY OBJECTIVE 10: DEFUSE BOMB 3

Order Bravo to Follow and then head through the doorway they were covering. This passage will lead down into a tunnel, which eventually will take you to the third and final Bomb. Even though you are on a tight time schedule, make sure you are cautious down here, as there are most likely one or two guards patrolling its length. Be extra cautious around corners, peeking around each one before moving on.

The tunnel ends at the base of Building E. As you come up the ramp, be wary of the row of windows above you. There might be a sentry inside its hallway and will get you in his sights if you're not careful. Building E is Spectrum's center of command, and the sentry will most likely come out to investigate once you are in the immediate area. Point your cross hairs over the door at the base of the ramp and order Bravo to Cover. They will keep tabs on the doorway and take care of any terrorists that come through this way.

There are a series of four oil tanks out here. The final Bomb is affixed to the back-right oil tank, which is to the left of the ramp you just came up from. If you have the time, clear out the immediate area of any terrorists you can find before attempting to defuse the Bomb. These include: a sniper stationed up on the right oil tower just behind the bomb, another two hiding behind the oil tower on the left, and a third off to the north, coming around the right side of Building E. There are likely a few more, on the other side of Building E and possibly coming from the tunnel to the left, but they shouldn't be a problem for you and Bravo.

Order Able to Defuse the final Bomb, and then help Bravo provide cover support while Boomer disarms it. Once it is defused, you will be able to concentrate on locating, restraining and rescuing the hostages.

43

TACMAP

SECONDARY OBJECTIVE 11: SECURE BUILDING E

The door to Building E is just in front of the tunnel ramp you came up from moments earlier. Once the final Bomb has been disarmed, head inside and Clear the building. There are two doors inside, one to your left, leading back outside and the other, to the right, leading down a hallway. You want the one to the right.

TACMAP

SECONDARY OBJECTIVE 12: LOCATE OIL WORKERS

There are four Oil Workers being held behind the left doorway marked "Authorized Personnel Only" at the end of the hallway. If you attempt to open the door, they will let you know they are alright. Since they are safe behind the locked door, you should leave them there and continue on.

PRIMARY OBJECTIVE 2: RESCUE HOSTAGES

TACMAP

The door straight ahead at the end of the hallway leads back outside. If you take an immediate left upon exiting the hallway, you will be facing east and looking directly at Building C. Head over to Building C and follow the ramp up to the second level.

HOSTAGES DOWN

You need to make sure the hostages aren't killed before you can rescue them. If the terrorists hear you coming, they will most likely execute them before you can reach them. Intel indicates that there are two hostages being held in separate rooms in the barracks in building C. Stealth and clean kills are especially critical here. If one enemy gets a shot off, the others will be alerted to your presence.

Before heading into Building C, point your cross hairs over the open doorway and Order Team to Ambush. They will move into the Building with you ready to remove any hostiles. Be ready for some serious opposition, as there are multiple terrorists holed up in the building guarding the hostages.

The first hostage is beyond the door to the left at the end of the hallway (just past the kitchen.) The hostage is most likely being watched by a lone guard. Your best bet is to enter and kill the guard quickly before he gets the opportunity to kill the hostage

The second hostage is being held around the corner in the room to the right. There are two doors here, both leading into the same room. Quickly pick a door and order Bravo to Bang/Clear. If you are quick enough, you should be able to get in and take out the guard before he can react. Make sure not to order them to Frag/Clear, as a Frag Grenade will surely kill both the enemy and the hostage in its blast.

45

TACMAP

SECONDARY OBJECTIVE 13: RESTRAIN WORKERS

It is standard operating procedure (SOP) to Restrain any hostages/civilians you come in contact with. This insures both their and your safety. Once the enemies have been neutralized and eliminated, Restrain the hostages by approaching them from behind and pressing the Action (✗) button when the "Restrain" icon appears.

SECONDARY OBJECTIVE 14: SECURE BUILDING C

TACMAP

Depending on how many terrorists you have eliminated inside Building C, there should be at least one or two more ready and waiting for you in the lounge area. This set of rooms is through the doorway across from where you rescued and restrained the second hallway. Cautiously Clear the room, and DO NOT stop to play a couple rounds of pool or a quick game on the coin-op before moving on.

The best exit out of Building C is through the doorway near the entrance, back toward the kitchen. If you head through the dining area, you'll find a shadowed corner that leads to a doorway. Exiting through this door will put you face-to-face with the Helipad.

SECONDARY OBJECTIVE 15: SECURE HELIPAD

TACMAP

The Helipad is to the southeast, around the opposite side of Building C. There are two sentries patrolling its borders. You can pick them off from afar, or you can climb up the surveying platform down to the right and snipe them from the higher vantage point. When you are sure they are neutralized, go up the ramp and officially secure the Helipad.

PRIMARY OBJECTIVE 3: SECURE OIL PLATFORM

TACMAP

By completing all of your mission objectives and eliminating the terrorist threat, you will have Secured the Oil Platform. Congratulations! That's another one for the good guys.

47

THAILAND: OPERATION GOOD KARMA
MISSION 4: GOLDEN TRIANGLE HOLIDAY

MISSION OVERVIEW:

"We have a new mission for you. Terrorists have acquired highly valuable biological data. We think they stole it from a Biotech smuggler out of Sri Lanka as he tried to cross the Straits of Malacca. The terrorists murdered him and his crew and then off-loaded the data; data that they are moving deep into the jungles of Thailand. Intercept these terrorists at their island waypoint before they move further upriver. Hopefully, you'll be there in time to retrieve the data."

OBJECTIVES

PRIMARY OBJECTIVES

1. SECURE OUTER ISLAND
2. PREVENT ENEMY ESCAPE
3. SECURE MAIN COMPLEX
4. RECLAIM BIO DATA

SECONDARY OBJECTIVES

1. Insert Via River
2. Eavesdrop for Intel
3. Eliminate Sentries
4. Search Hut for Intel
5. Bravo to Juliet
6. Clear Hut One
7. Clear Hut Two
8. Breach Final Hut
9. Move to Zulu

TACMAP

PRIMARY OBJECTIVE 1: SECURE OUTER ISLAND

The Riddah Rouge has set up camp on a series of small islands across a shallow river. The first outer island is where you will be inserted into the mission. It's imperative you're not seen until you've been able to gather a bit of intelligence from the enemy, which can only be done by crawling under the hut they are occupying and eavesdropping. If you are heard or spotted, your opportunity will be blown. Once you have heard everything you need, you and your SEAL team members must eliminate and neutralize the sentries posted on the outer island, without letting any terrorists escape, and locate any Intel that might have been left behind. This objective will not be fulfilled until you kill or restrain all enemies on the outer island.

TACMAP

SECONDARY OBJECTIVE 1: INSERT VIA RIVER

Your first objective is to insert yourself and your fellow SEAL team members into the mission without being seen. There are a series of grassy hides along the river which will provide cover.

ENVIRONMENTAL COVER

Oftentimes, you will have to make use of the environment and your surroundings. In addition to shadows and darkness, organic objects, such as foliage, water and rain, can provide extra cover and camouflage, making it tough for the enemy to spot you. When hiding and whenever possible, assume the Crouch or Prone position and stay as motionless as possible until the enemy has turned away. This will lessen your chances of being discovered.

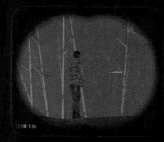
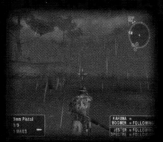
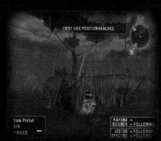

One of the Riddah Rouge is patrolling the island periphery, directly in front of you. Since you don't know exactly how many sentries are patrolling the island's perimeter yet, it's best not to kill him. Instead, equip your Binoculars and watch him until he has his back turned to you.

As soon as he turns away, quickly run to the first grassy hide, diagonally to the right. Make sure you are in the Crouch position and are well-hidden behind the foliage when you get there. Stop and re-equip your Binoculars and repeat the process. You will have to continue this game of Cat and Mouse for a few more minutes. The moment he turns his back and is no longer facing in the direction of you and your team members, head to the second grassy hide diagonally to the right. There is a third hide just beyond the second, again diagonally to the right. Be patient and wait for him to look the other way before running to it. The area of insertion is the north corner of the island, just diagonally to the right of the third hide. When you get to its muddy wall, you will have completed your first objective.

TACMAP

SECONDARY OBJECTIVE 2: EAVESDROP FOR INTEL

Before you move any further, take a moment to locate the enemies patrolling the island. With your Binoculars equipped, you should be able to spot at least three guards patrolling the perimeter. Your next objective is to crawl under the hut directly to the north and eavesdrop for Intel — a feat much harder than it sounds.

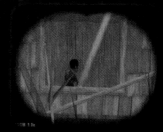

Order Bravo to Hold Position — the less movement the better — and then take a few moments to carefully watch the comings and goings of the guards. When it looks like all is clear, make a dash for the grassy hide just in front of the island facing the hut. Before heading under the hut, be wary of the window on its side. If you are seen by the enemy inside, your cover will be blown and you won't be able to obtain any information. Assume the Prone position and crawl under the hut when you are absolutely sure no guards are looking your way.

CMAP

SECONDARY OBJECTIVE 3: ELIMINATE SENTRIES

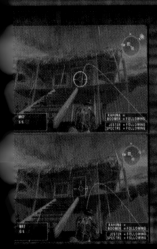

 As soon as you have gathered the Intel, order Bravo to Follow and then order them to Fire at Will. Locate all three sentries (which shouldn't be too difficult a task, since they will most likely have already sought you out) and eliminate them. Be careful not to let any of them escape, as it's possible they will choose to run instead of fight, blowing your Primary Objective in the process and prematurely alerting the terrorists on the main island of your presence. When engaging in a fire fight, make sure to use the island's trees and foliage for cover and protection.

There are a few more terrorists inside the hut. There are a variety of ways to safely take them out. You can order Bravo or Able to Bang/Clear or Flash/Clear or an even more satisfying way is to lob a Grenade through one of the hut's openings.

LOBBING GRENADES

When you have the luxury of stealth and surprise, you can opt to throw/lob a Grenade at unsuspecting enemies. Judging the distance, arc and power of your throw is super-simple. When you want to throw a Grenade, select it from your Weapons Cache to equip it, then press and hold down the Attack (R1) button. The harder you hold down the R1 button, the farther the Grenade will travel. The Grenade's path is represented by a yellow arc, which will increase and decrease depending on how hard or soft you are pressing the R1 button. The power of your throw is represented by a yellow circular meter around your cross hairs. The harder you press down on the meter, the more the meter will fill. Make sure you are not too close to the landing point of the Grenade, as it's entirely possible to kill yourself in its blast radius.

CMAP

SECONDARY OBJECTIVE 4: SEARCH HUT FOR INTEL

The one and only hut on the Outer Island has a Folder that might hold some valuable intelligence. As soon as the hut has been secured, venture up and inside. Sitting on the small desk is the Folder. Quickly grab it and get ready to move on.

51

TACMAP

SECONDARY OBJECTIVE 5: BRAVO TO JULIET

As soon as the Rouge is aware of your presence, they will head for the docks and try to flee via a pair of boats. It's imperative you do not let them get away. In order to stop them from escaping, you will have to destroy the boats with two well-placed C-4 charges. Getting to the docks is another matter entirely, as there are many terrorists between you and your goal. Time is definitely an issue, but you will still have to be careful and cautious to get there in one piece.

You could attempt to head straight to the docks, which are located between Nav points Romeo and Juliet. In doing so, you will encounter tough resistance and, most likely, allow a few enemies to escape. Instead, follow the path, which will take you through Nav points Delta, Echo and Foxtrot along the way.

As you set out, be sure to order Bravo to Run To Juliet, as they will cover you and provide back up fire when you arrive. Also double check that you have ordered your Team to Fire At Will.

TACMAP

PRIMARY OBJECTIVE 2: PREVENT ENEMY ESCAPE

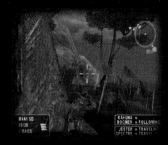

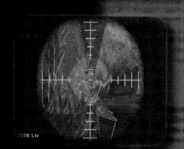

While Bravo is heading off to Nav point Juliet, you need to be on the move as well. Keep your long-range rifle equipped and head out toward Nav point Delta. Make sure you frequently refer to your TACMAP to stay on track, as the river is large and flooded, making it easy to get off track.

You will meet opposition at each and every island along the way. Use the natural environment for cover and keep an eye out for any hostiles. You most likely won't be able to sneak up on them, but you should at least be able to pick a few off from a safe distance.

Be especially cautious when entering the water between islands. The terrorists will use their numbers and added protection of the water level to make it harder to see and hit them.

If they feel threatened or overwhelmed, they will retreat and make for the docks. Try not to let any get away and make every shot count. If a few do flee from the area, keep an eye on the timer that appears on the right side of the screen — you will only have a short 45 seconds to disable the boats and keep them from escaping.

Hopefully, Bravo made it to Juliet without too much of a struggle and are waiting for you when you get there. From their vantage point, they will be able to provide covering fire while you head for the two boats and take care of business. Equip your C-4 from your Weapons Cache when you get the boats in sight and then attach one explosive to each. As soon as the boats are destroyed, you will have completed the objective.

PRIMARY OBJECTIVE 3: SECURE MAIN COMPLEX

TACMAP

The main complex is comprised of the docks (where you just wreaked havoc) and a few huts. Hut One is the primary hut, which is where the Riddah Rouge officers are stationed. Hut One houses two separate rooms across from each other, and there are most likely one or two officers in each. Hut Two is just north and beyond Hut One. Hut Two is much smaller (similar to the one you Cleared on the Outer Island) and should be easier to secure. You will also have to eliminate any terrorists who might be outside of the huts. This objective will only be accomplished once you have secured the two huts.

SECONDARY OBJECTIVE 6: CLEAR HUT ONE

TACMAP

Before you attempt to Clear and Secure Hut One, order Bravo to Run To Whiskey. Nav point Whiskey is the perfect position to keep any enemies from trying to escape via the exit. As soon as they arrive and are in a Holding position, Clear the hut by either stealthfully approaching and entering its rooms, or lobbing Grenades through its doorways and windows, then entering and cleaning up the mess. Either way, make sure you search the rooms after you've eliminated any hostiles.

TACMAP

SECONDARY OBJECTIVE 7: CLEAR HUT TWO

Hut Two is just behind and to the right of Hut One. Once Hut One has been Secured, you can hop down from the back exit and head to Hut Two. Again, it's easier to lob a Grenade into the hut than try to enter it first, giving the enemy an unnecessary advantage. If you have run out of Grenades, you can order either Able or Bravo to Deploy either Bang or Frag Grenades by pointing your cross hairs over the open doorway or window. Make sure to enter and search the hut before moving on in order to complete the Secondary Objective. You should have completed Primary Objective 3 as well.

ZOOM: 3.0x

SECONDARY OBJECTIVE 8: BREACH FINAL HUT

TACMAP

There is one final hut, directly off to the north, where the Bio Data is said to be kept. In order to reclaim the Bio Data, you will have to first Breach and Secure the hut. Make sure your Team is ordered to Follow and move out to the north. There is a muddy path along the ground that will take you directly to the final hut. You can follow it if you like, but be sure to use the boulders, foliage and trees for protection and cover along the way.

When you get the hut in your sights, make sure to keep out of the enemy's line of sight through its open door and windows. Get as close as possible without alerting the enemy to your presence, point your cross hairs over the doorway, and then Order Team to Bang/Clear. Boomer, Jester and Spectre will work together to Breach the final hut and eliminate the terrorist inside.

PRIMARY OBJECTIVE 4: RECLAIM BIO DATA

When the smoke settles, head up and into the hut to search for the Bio Data. The Riddah Rouge were kind enough to leave it sitting on the desk. Unfortunately, the Bio Data you're looking for is not with the documents you've found. The Rouge must have moved it somewhere up the river.

TACMAP

SECONDARY OBJECTIVE 9: MOVE TO ZULU

TACMAP

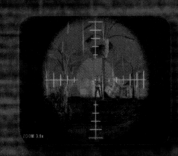

Since you've completed your Primary Objectives, it's time to move you and your SEAL team members to the Extraction Point at Nav Point Zulu.

Zulu is off to the north east, a little further up the river. It's a good bet you will meet heavy resistance along the way. Work slowly and cautiously toward the Nav point, scanning the area for hostiles as you go.

When you reach Nav point Zulu, hold your ground and stay in the general vicinity until the rest of your team members arrive. When you are all together, the helicopter will descend and extract you from the mission.

THAILAND: OPERATION GOOD KARMA
MISSION 5: TEMPLE AT HOHN KAEN

MISSION OVERVIEW:

"We don't have time to worry about the loss of the Bio Data. The Riddah Rouge has taken captive the U.S. Ambassador to Thailand and his wife. The terrorists have demanded ransom money and threaten to execute the hostages if their demands are not met. Intelligence tracked their movements to an abandoned Temple in the jungles of Hohn Kaen. You're their last hope for survival. Good luck, team."

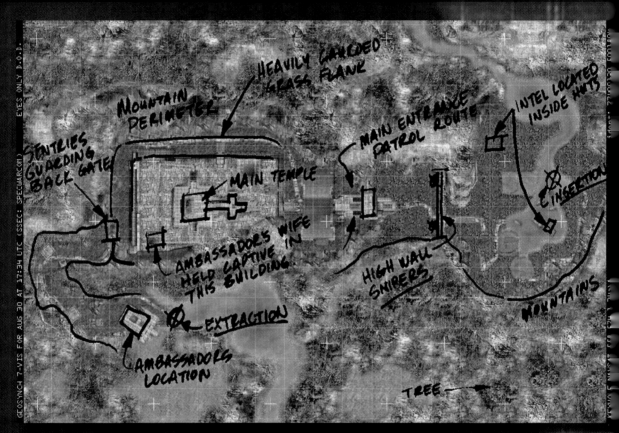

OBJECTIVES

PRIMARY OBJECTIVES

1. CLEAR INSERTION AREA
2. SECURE FLANK
3. SECURE WIFE
4. CLEAR TEMPLE AREA
5. HELICOPTER EXTRACTION
6. SECURE AMBASSADOR

SECONDARY OBJECTIVES

1. Eavesdrop on Locals
2. Identify Sentries
3. Ambush Flank Guards

TACMAP

PRIMARY OBJECTIVE 1: CLEAR INSERTION AREA

Satellite data shows that there are at least six sentries guarding the insertion area, making a stealth entry tough, but not impossible. You won't be able to clear the entire area until you've gathered some Intel from the locals, who will go quiet if they hear any commotion outside of their huts. Luckily, the dense foliage and thick brush will help in keeping you relatively hidden from the enemy's view.

There are a few guards just yards from your drop point. Leave Bravo in their Holding position for the moment and sneak past them, heading west, while keeping the cover of the large boulders to the right of you. Your goal is to make it around the second large boulder where there is an enemy hiding in the darkness. Take him out with a silent kill before he can alert any others to your presence. If you're patient enough, you just might be able to catch him relieving himself. Give him a good boot to the head in mid-stream.

While he was urinating on the bushes, two more sentries walked by, heading down the stone pathway to the right. Go back the way you came and stealthfully move around the opposite boulder. The first guard should be right around this grassy area, with his back to you. Take him out silently.

The second guard should have walked down the pathway to the water's edge. Quickly sneak up behind him before he can turn around and eliminate him as well.

TACMAP

SECONDARY OBJECTIVE 1: EAVESDROP ON LOCALS

That leaves three sentries left, but you won't be killing them (and completing your Primary Objective) until you've gathered some Intel on the Ambassador and his wife. There are two huts in the area, one not far off to the west, and another up on the hill to the northeast. You need to get close enough to them to be able to overhear any valuable information the locals might have.

Stay close to the water's edge and stealthfully follow it to the west until you are underneath the large hut. Move slowly and silently, keeping an eye on the guard stationed on the boat in the middle of the water. If he happens to turn your way, remain still and wait for him to turn away again. Use the scope on your Night Vision Goggles to get a closer view, if you can't tell which way he's facing. When you get underneath the hut, stay crouched in the water, keeping the large wooden panels of the boat between you and the guard, and eavesdrop on the locals inside.

As soon as you have confirmation their conversation is over, quietly head up out of the water and back to the stone path. Make your way back toward where you killed the guard by the water, and then slowly crouch walk to the small island in the middle, using its height for cover. You want to keep from being seen, especially by the guard on the boat. Stay low and keep him in your sights. If he happens to turn your way, stop moving until he turns around again. When his back is to you, make for the covered boat, which is diagonally to the right.

There is another guard on patrol on the other side of the water. His route takes him from the hut up on the hill to your right, and then back down along the stone path. He will stop about halfway up the path and then head back the other way. You want to wait and catch him from behind silently with a stealth kill as he heads up the hill toward the hut. Remember to keep an eye on the guard in the boat and only make your move when he is turned the other way.

The second hut is just up the hill to the east. Quietly make your way through the rice paddy and get close enough to listen in on the local's conversation. When they stop talking, you will have gathered the required Intel, completing your objective.

Before leaving the area, you still need to eliminate the remaining guards. Since you no longer need to worry about making a little noise, why not call in some support? Order Support to Sweep and an attack Helo will come hovering overhead and pepper the area with gunfire.

CALLING IN SUPPORT

Depending on the mission parameters, you will occasionally have the opportunity to Call in an attack Helicopter for covering fire Support and Extraction. When this option is available, it will show up in your Command Menu. When you order Support to Sweep, the Helicopter will come into the area and spread cover fire, eliminating any terrorists out in the open and giving you a much-needed breather. When you have a secured hostage who needs to be air lifted out of the area, the Command "Extract" will become available.

To finish off Clearing the insertion area, you will need to take out the remaining guard. He's equipped with a sniper rifle and is stationed inside the ramshackle building up the pathway to the west. If you're quick enough, you can sneak up on him and take him out with a head shot during the Support Sweep (he should retreat outside and start shooting at the Helo) — he will most likely be too busy attacking the Helo to even notice you. Or, if you wait, he will go back into the shack and return to his post facing the window to the south. Either way, he is easy prey.

PRIMARY OBJECTIVE 2: SECURE FLANK

TACMAP

The flank of the temple is heavily guarded. Try to eliminate guards silently to avoid alerting any terrorists of your presence.

You have a long way to go before you will be able to secure the Flank of the Temple, which is heavily guarded. The Flank is where the Temple entrance is located, and you will need to eliminate all of the guards patrolling its perimeter if you are going to get inside and rescue the Ambassador's wife. Before you can even think of completing this objective, you will first need to make your way over to the Flank. The path is filled with patrolling guards and snipers, so stealth will be a major requirement if you want to try to even the odds.

Start by ordering Bravo to Follow, then head up the stone path and follow it up the mountainside to the east. You will approach the first Temple wall, which leads into a large clearing. Don't even think about taking the stairs through the entrance; it's most likely heavily guarded and you will find yourself caught in a crossfire when you come out the other end. Instead, move up the hill to the right of the stairs, and follow the Temple wall to the right until you come to a small opening.

Equip your Night Vision Goggles and slowly and quietly head into the opening. It turns into a small tunnel which leads through the wall. When you come out on the other side, you will find a sentry with his back to you, guarding the stairway entrance. Crouch walk up to him silently and eliminate him.

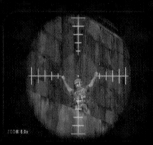
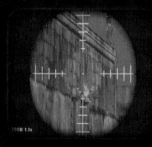

There are snipers up on the wall and, if you were to move out into the open, they would make quick work of you and your SEAL team members. Quietly climb up to the foliage on the small mound to your right and use it for cover. Get a bead on the one to the left first and snipe him, then take out the second. Before leaving your vantage point, scope the area to see if you can find a patrolling sentry or two.

If none are in sight, climb back down and slowly make your way around the dark path between the mountain wall and the mound to the northwest. There is another sentry crouched down just around the corner. He may or may not be aware of your presence, so move slowly and deliberately and take him down.

There are at least two more terrorists in the immediate area. If you didn't take out the patrolling guard, keep an eye out for him. There should also be another around the mountain wall to the right. Order your Team to Fire at Will and clear the area of any remaining enemies, including any that might be approaching from the far Temple entrance.

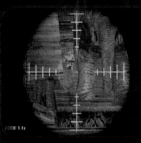

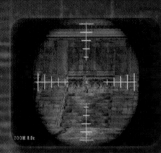

When you feel confident that you have secured the clearing, make for the next Temple entrance to the north. You won't have the luxury of a hidden tunnel this time, so stealth is even more important here. Stay to the walls, using anything you can to keep you and your SEAL team members hidden, as well as for cover from possible enemy fire. There are two openings inside the Temple wall which lead to a second clearing. The one to the right is lit with an incense candle, which throws enough light to betray your presence. The right opening is dark and shadowed — definitely the way to go.

There is a small alcove inside the opening; quickly duck inside and use the wall for cover. Peeking out from here, you should be able to spot one or two sentries making their rounds. Use the elephant statue to the right as a landmark and keep your sights trained toward that general area. Using your scope, you should be able to take out a few of the terrorists before they are aware of you. If things get a little hairy, lob a Grenade or two in their general direction to even things out. There should be a final guard stationed on the steps far off across the bridge.

The Flank of the Temple is across the bridge and to the right. Crossing the bridge will leave you wide open to any enemies that you might have missed or are hiding. A better choice is to hop down into the water to the left of the bridge and slowly make your way across to the other side. Stay alert and use the environment for cover whenever you can. When you get to the other side, stay on the path and follow it to the east toward the Flank.

SECONDARY OBJECTIVE 2: IDENTIFY SENTRIES

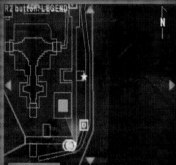

Before you move to the Temple Flank, stop at the corner wall and take a quick peek. There is a crumbling wall a few yards off to the north that could provide you with much needed cover, as well as give you the opportunity to see what you are up against. Make sure the coast is clear and then make a quick dash for it.

When you get to the crumbling wall, equip your Night Vision Goggles and slowly peek out down the path. There are at least four sentries patrolling the path along the Flank's perimeter. You need to get your sights on each one to complete the objective. In order to gain entrance into the Temple and complete your Primary and Secondary Objectives, you are also going to need to eliminate them all as quietly as possible. Get ready to move into action as soon as you get a visual confirmation.

TACMAP

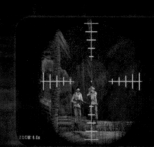

SECONDARY OBJECTIVE 3: AMBUSH FLANK GUARDS

You can attempt to get closer by making another dash for either the small wall to the left or the columns to the right, or you can stay put and snipe as many as possible. Either way, there is no way to eliminate them all without letting them know you're here. With Able and Bravo helping out, you should be able to neutralize them without too much trouble. A Flash Grenade is particularly helpful if you want to temporarily stun the enemies to gain the upper hand.

SECONDARY OBJECTIVE 4: SECURE WIFE

TACMAP

The Temple entrance is to the left, along the Flank. This is the only way into the Temple grounds, so you have no choice but to take it. Head up the small stairs, and HQ will give you a quick reminder that Morgan, the Ambassador's Wife, is in danger. You need to keep your mind on the mission objectives. But, before rescuing her from the Rouge, you should first clear the Temple Area of any hostiles, making it less of a chance she will be hit by enemy fire.

Don't head straight into the Temple grounds, as there is a shadowed walkway that winds its way around the atrium, giving you an opportunity to stay unseen for a few more minutes. Follow it around to the right, and stop short when the path opens up to the grounds. There is a sniper stationed off to the northwest, and you can pick him off before he even knows what hit him. Use this vantage point to scope out any other potential targets that might be patrolling the Temple grounds. Continue down the walkway and follow it around the corner to the left until it leads out onto the Temple grounds. The Ambassador's wife is located in the small structure to the southwest (there is an elephant statue and four palm trees next to it).

The Intel gathered suggests she is lightly guarded. Her safety is a main concern, and you don't want to give the terrorists any opportunity to kill her once you start clearing the area. Quietly make your way around the back side of the structure, and sneak up to the doorway from the side. Point your cross hairs over the doorway and order your Team to Bang / Clear. They will Breach the structure and eliminate the two guards inside without harming Morgan. When it's safe, Restrain and leave her inside the structure, where she will be safe for the time being. There are still many terrorists within the Temple Grounds and you don't want to take the chance of her getting hit by hostile fire.

PRIMARY OBJECTIVE 4: CLEAR TEMPLE AREA

TACMAP

Head back out onto the Temple grounds and slowly and deliberately head south, hugging the far right wall, toward the main Temple in the middle. Keep an eye out for any terrorists on the way. It's a good idea to equip your Night Vision Goggles inside, as the Temple is bathed in darkness, making it tough to spot any potential targets.

The Temple is shaped like a large "T" with a long corridor that runs down the middle. You should have entered from the top end, where the huge Buddha statue is located. Use the jutting walls for cover along with your Night Vision Goggles and peek out down the hallway. There should be at least one guard patrolling its length, with possibly two more somewhere in the immediate vicinity.

When you have cleared the Temple, move down the corridor and head back out onto the Temple grounds. There should only be one or two sentries remaining, patrolling along its perimeter. Take it slow and easy and locate and eliminate them. Objective accomplished.

SECONDARY OBJECTIVE 5: HELICOPTER EXTRACTION

It's time to extract Morgan from the area. The extraction zone is right in front of the entrance to the Temple grounds from which you entered. Unfortunately, this is the only area large enough for the Helo to land, which is also wide open and susceptible to enemy fire.

Point your cross hairs over the entrance and order Bravo to Cover Area (you might need to point toward the ground to get them to confirm). They will take position and guard the entrance while you retrieve Morgan. They should be enough of a force to stop any terrorists from getting through.

Head back into the structure and order Morgan to Follow. When you come back out, lend Bravo a hand and help eliminate any enemies that have attempted an assault. Make sure to keep an eye out for any enemies coming from other directions as well.

When you have cleared the area, lead Morgan to the middle of the extraction zone which is at Nav point Zulu (also indicated by a large "X" on your radar and TACMAP screen).

When you are in position, call on the Helo once more, this time ordering Support to Extract. The Helicopter will fly in and hastily land, allowing Morgan to get on board before extracting her from the site. One down, one to go.

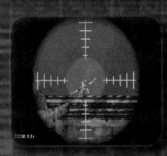

TACMAP

PRIMARY OBJECTIVE 5: SECURE AMBASSADOR

Now to find and secure the Ambassador. Intelligence places him due west, somewhere around Nav point Romeo. The Temple should be cleared of all enemies, allowing you to head out through the main entrance along the Flank. In order to exit, you'll have to climb up to the ledge.

On the other side, continue following the path along Flank north. You shouldn't encounter any resistance until you turn the corner along the back end of the Temple wall.

Be especially cautious of the sniper on the far west wall. He is a dead aim and will get you in his sights if you give him the chance. The best strategy for dealing with him is to assume the Prone position and crawl to the elephant statue directly in front of you. Using it for cover, you should be able to peek out from this position and pick him off before he can do the same to you.

As soon as you clear the immediate area, continue along the path through the wall and around the corners. Make sure to continue using stealth and the environment for cover as you go. There is another sentry around the third corner, guarding the small opening in the wall.

You'll find a small ravine on the other side, cluttered with stone structures — a perfect place for an ambush. Go slow and sweep the area cautiously. Use the thick foliage and building walls for cover and protection as you move forward.

If you move to the right side of the ravine, you should be able to climb up on the back of the right-hand structure's ledge (from a Standing position), where you will be able to clip the terrorist standing guard from behind through the window without alerting him to your presence. There is at least one more sentry patrolling the immediate area.

This next roofless structure takes up most of the path, but you can squeeze by on the left side, rather than going through its middle. Hug the left mountain wall and stay in the shadows. There is a sentry up on the wall a few yards off. He may or may not be aware of your presence, so use caution when peeking out from cover to locate him.

Stay to the left and take the left-most entrance under the wall. Use the large building for cover and attempt to locate the next set of hostiles. There are at least three patrolling in the immediate area.
The Ambassador is located in the building at the end of the ravine. There is at least one guard inside, and another two on the roof. You should be able to snipe at least one of the rooftop guards at a distance from the outside.

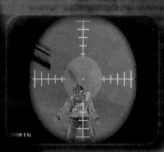

Approach the building from either side. It sounds like you've arrived just in time. Things are getting a little dicey for the Ambassador. Order Bravo to Ambush, and they will prepare to light it up. Before entering the building, use the outer wall for cover and try to eliminate the guard on the ground.
If you left one on the roof, you'll find he is particularly tough, as he is wielding a semi-automatic rifle, giving you very little breathing room to take aim and eliminate him. Use the large stone planters at the entrance for cover and quickly take them out when it is safe.

As soon as the building is secure, head down the stairs and Restrain the Ambassador. Doing so will accomplish your final mission objective, allowing you and your fellow SEAL team members to get out. Mission accomplished!

MISSION 6: CITY OF THE FORGOTTEN

MISSION OVERVIEW:

"The Riddah Rouge must be stopped. While no ransom was paid for Ambassador Ness, Thongkon's personal fortune may have allowed the Riddah Rouge to manufacture a small amount of Biological Agent. The Thai government is becoming increasingly agitated by this threat of biological terrorism on their soil. You can stop the Riddah Rouge permanently. Capture Thongkon, and retrieve the biological agents and data. And remember, while these men are dangerous, so are you."

OBJECTIVES

PRIMARY OBJECTIVES	SECONDARY OBJECTIVES
1 RECON INSERTION AREA	1 ID Patrols with NVG
2 SECURE RIVERBANK	2 Eliminate Patrols
3 SECURE COMPOUND	3 Infiltrate Temple
4 PREVENT LEADER ESCAPE	4 Restrain Leader
5 OBTAIN INTEL	5 Blow Door with C-4
6 SECURE SUB LEVEL	6 Contain Enemy
7 OBTAIN BIO AGENT	

TACMAP

SECONDARY OBJECTIVE 1: ID PATROLS WITH NIGHT VISION GOGGLES

Your insertion point for the mission is at the edge of a riverbank, which will take you around a mountainous area and into a clearing. At the end of the clearing is a series of ancient ruins the Riddah Rouge is using for their base of operations. The key is getting to this compound as quietly as possible, using mainly stealth kills and silenced weapons, as the leader is already feeling your heat and will likely attempt to escape if he knows you're here. The first objective you will meet is Identifying the patrols with your Night Vision Goggles.

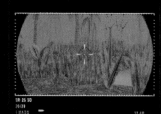

The river is crawling with sentries patrolling its bank, making it slow going. But, thankfully, there is a tremendous amount of brush and foliage, as well as thick fog, which helps to provide almost total cover. Equip your Night Vision Goggles and stay in the Crouch position. Besides allowing you to see in the darkness, the Night Vision Goggles also magnify your field of vision a bit, making it easier to spot the enemy. You are going to have to move slowly and deliberately from bush to bush as you follow the riverbank to the east.

 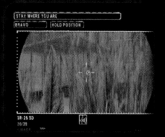 

You most likely won't encounter any resistance until you arrive at the first hut. Stop short of the hut and order Bravo to Hold Position. You'll find two guards inside having a heated conversation regarding Thongkon and the imminent arrival of "the Americans" (that's you!). Un-equip the Night Vision Goggles, hang back at the bottom of the ramp, and wait for one of the guards to leave the hut. He will stop at the edge above for a moment — don't let him spot you. When he moves around the side of the hut, you need to spring into action.

Quickly go up the ramp and inside the hut, using surprise to take out the first guard inside with a Rifle Butt to the head. As soon as he goes down, exit the hut and follow the other guard around the corner. With any luck, his back will be turned to you and you can rush up and execute a repeat performance. If you were quick enough and quiet enough, none of the other guards patrolling the riverbank will be aware of you and your SEAL team members. But, if you allowed an enemy to get a shot off, your cover will be blown and you won't be able to complete the objective.

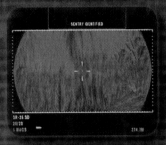 Head back down to the riverbank and re-equip your Night Vision Goggles. Order Bravo to Follow, then continue your slow trek through the brush. Constantly sweep the area from left to right as you go. It helps to have the Aim Assist option turned on during this portion of the mission (you can switch it on and off via the pause menu), as a red square will appear over an enemy when you have him in your cross hairs, giving you a visual confirmation of his whereabouts. There are a total of four sentries you have to ID along the riverbank.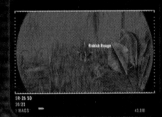

SECONDARY OBJECTIVE 2: ELIMINATE PATROLS

 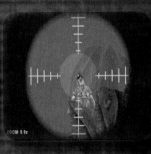 

TACMAP

When you ID an enemy, stay Crouched or hidden in the Prone position and follow his movement. When he is close enough, either take him out with a stealth kill or use your SR-25 SD's scope for a clean head shot. If you miss though, he will alert the others with his radio — blowing your objective.

The fourth and last sentry is patrolling somewhere around the second hut you come across. When you get him in your sights and squeeze, your objective will be accomplished.

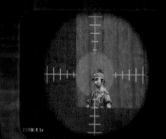

PRIMARY OBJECTIVE 1: RECON INSERTION AREA

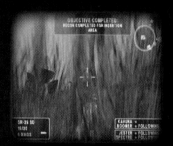

Your Primary Objective is to reach Nav Point Charlie without being detected, using reconnaissance and stealth along the way. You should be well over half way there by now, and have killed off most of the opposition as well. Before moving farther down the bank, check and see if the hut is occupied. Instead of heading up the ramp, move up the hillside a bit to get a better view and take a look in the window. If someone's inside, eliminate him with a well-placed head shot.

It's just a few more yards to the Nav Point and objective completion. Stay low and keep to the brush. You're only just getting started.

PRIMARY OBJECTIVE 2: SECURE RIVERBANK

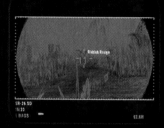

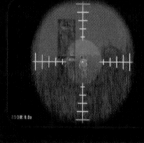

As you round the mountainside and get closer to the compound, you will encounter another group of sentries patrolling the riverbank. It's imperative you neutralize them, leaving no one alive. Re-equip your Night Vision Goggles and continue along the bank.

It's a good idea to stop frequently while in the Crouch position and scan the tall grass for any hostiles. When you get one in your sights, only take the shot if you are confident it will be an instant kill. There are approximately four sentries patrolling this area, but more may come if they hear any gunfire exchanges.

TACMAP

PRIMARY OBJECTIVE 3: SECURE COMPOUND

You are going to want to enter the main Compund from its north, right-most side. It is heavily guarded, so go slowly. Intelligence puts the Riddah Rouge leader, Thongkon (a.k.a. Bad Dog), somewhere inside the Temple, which is located at back end of the Compound to the west. Before you can even get to him, you will have to go through his small army.

Before heading up, take a moment to survey the Compound and see if you can spot any guards patrolling its perimeter. You might be able to catch one along the wall near the right set of stairs.

It's likely that you alerted one or two more guards who are camped just up and to the right of those stairs. Sit tight for a moment and see if they come barrelling down the stairs, making themselves easy targets for you and your teammates. If not, use caution as you ascend the stairs. The camp is just to the right of the stairs.

Follow the Compound's perimeter wall to the left. Stick to the shadows and use its decrepit walls for cover from enemy fire.

Continue down the perimeter, staying close to the wall to your right as you go. When you get to the front side of the Compound, peek around the wall and see if you can spot any sentries. There should be one or two patrolling the immediate area, and another should come down the stairs off in the distance to your right when he hears the commotion. Stay alert and keep your eyes open for any movement.

Climb (which are marked by two huge elephant statues on either side) the stairs when you reach the center of the Compound. There is a huge chamber at the top with a giant Buddha statue in its center. There is also one or two guards stationed inside who are more than likely aware of your presence. Take cover and pick them off as soon as you can. If given the chance, they will yell to alert others. When they go down, you should have secured the Compound and completed Primary Objective 3.

TACMAP

SECONDARY OBJECTIVE 3: INFILTRATE TEMPLE

You need to keep Thongkon from escaping. As soon as he knows you're here, he will make a break for the river. To force Thongkon to surrender, you must separate him from his bodyguards. Also, it's imperative you apprehend him before he can see the river, as the closer he is to escaping, the less likely he is to surrender.

Unfortunately, Thongkon is located a ways off inside the Temple, and will have made sure there are many guards blocking the way between you and him. First you will need to make your way over to Nav Point Echo, which is back down the stairs and due south of your current position.

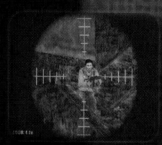

If the enemy is on to you, they will come running, guns raised and ready to shoot, out of the entrance at Nav Point Echo. Listen for their war cries and stay put to pick them off. If they aren't aware, you will be able to eavesdrop on their conversation, and then stealthfully take them out from the cover of the corner. Either way, they have to be eliminated.

You can also make use of a well-thrown AN-M8 Smoke Grenade, which will confuse the enemy and give you a chance to take them out before they even know what hit them. If you don't have any in your Weapons Cache, point your cross hairs over the opening and order Bravo to Deploy Smoke.

Make sure you refer to your TACMAP for the best path to the Temple. There are many ruins and small structures littered about the Compound, making it easy to become turned around. It's a good idea to order Bravo to Fire at Will, as you'll likely encounter many more guards along the way. Always remember to stick to the shadows, and don't forget to use the environment for cover as well. When you get close to the Pyramid-shaped Temple, take a moment to scan its perimeter with your scope (especially the stairs) and see if you can locate one or two terrorists.

When all is relatively clear, move on, but NOT up the front stairs. Instead, stay to the left of the Temple and enter through its side entrance. Once inside, you will have infiltrated its interior, getting you one step closer to Thongkon and the Biological Agent.

TACMAP

PRIMARY OBJECTIVE 4: PREVENT LEADER ESCAPE

While there is nothing remarkable about this petty terrorist, his distinguishable features include a turban and an eye patch. HQ wants him brought in alive if at all possible but, if need be, the use of deadly force is authorized.

Thongkon is inside and most likely already planning his escape. He is highly unstable and also completely unpredictable, making it tough to know which way he will run and what actions he will take. He is more brave with his bodyguards and fellow terrorists around him, and will be aggressive as long as they are there to protect and back him up.

GENERAL STRATEGIES FOR SECURING BAD DOG

There is a set of stairs to your right, which lead up to the main floor of the Temple. You'll have a much easier time picking off his bodyguards from this vantage point, rather than trying a frontal assault.

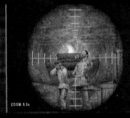

ZOOM 8.0x

It's possible to pick off his body guards quickly (even if Thongkon gets by you), but if and when he gets outside, there will be more terrorists waiting to protect him. If you have to, you can leave Thongkon alone momentarily, and take them out as soon as you can, but make sure you don't lose sight of which exit he takes and DON'T mistakingly kill him in the heat of the battle.

As soon as Thongkon's bodyguards have been eliminated, getting him to surrender will be an easier prospect. Chase him down and don't let him get too far ahead of you. You can attempt to wound him by shooting him in the leg or abdomen, but definitely do not aim for the head.

Flash or Smoke Grenades also have an effect, although you will have to order one of your SEAL team members to Deploy Bang and aim your cross hairs in the direction you think Thongkon will be running, making it a tricky proposition. If you can, order them to Deploy Flash Bang before he starts running, confusing him and his body guards and providing cover for you and your SEAL team members.

He might also choose to fight, shooting at you and your team members and even throw a Grenade or two your way. Keep your gun trained on him and don't get too close, he's very aggressive and will not hesitate to butt you in the head with his rifle.

Eventually, he will give up the fight and surrender. Even after he surrenders, keep an eye out for any hostiles that are still in the area. It seems like there's always one or two that will engage you and your SEAL team members when you attempt to Restrain Thongkon.

TACMAP

SECONDARY OBJECTIVE 4: RESTRAIN LEADER

Restrain him as soon as he surrenders, and leave him face down, on the ground, for extraction. Good job, although you still have to track down the Bio Data and the Bio Agent, which are somewhere in the Temple.

Be careful not to let your guard down. Even though he might be restrained, his followers will keep up the fight. Watch your back and double check your Team is ordered to Fire at Will.

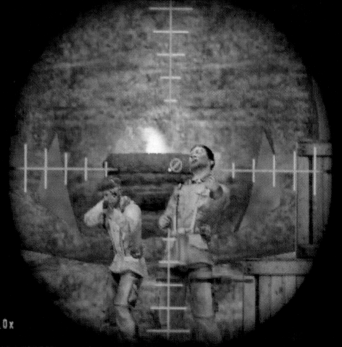

ZOOM: 8.0x

PRIMARY OBJECTIVE 5: OBTAIN INTEL

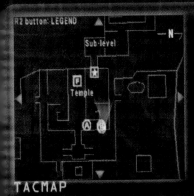

TACMAP

In his haste to escape, Thongkon left a Binder with the Bio Data Intelligence behind. It is located upstairs on the main floor of the Temple. If you make your way over there, you will find it sitting on a ledge, to the right of the lit Buddha statue. Grab it and it's yours.

SECONDARY OBJECTIVE 5: BLOW DOOR WITH C-4

TACMAP

The Temple has a sub-level directly underneath its massive structure. The door leading down to the sub-level has been boarded up to block access below. A well-placed C-4 charge should do the job. The door is located down the opposite set of stairs, on the right side of the Temple.

Choose the C-4 from your Weapons Cache and attach it to the doorway, but be ready for whoever might be waiting for you on the other side.

Prepare to throw an AN-M8 Smoke Grenade through the doorway as soon as it's cleared. This will fill the room below with smoke, confusing any enemies inside and giving you the upper hand.

PRIMARY OBJECTIVE 6: SECURE SUB-LEVEL

TACMAP

Things are about to get a bit hairy when you go through the sub-level doorway. There are many terrorists down here, presumably guarding Thongkon's Bio Agent stash. You should be able to get the drop on the few who are currently choking on the smoke fumes.

The next small room below leads into the sub-level's interior. Be very cautious as there are at least four to five enemies in the immediate area. They are aware of your presence and will come running through the doorways ready to fire. This is a particularly tough area to clear; the enemies have become very aggressive and they will attempt to overcome you and your teammates. Caution and accuracy are required to stay healthy down here. By the time you make it into the interior, you should have encountered and eliminated the threat and secured the area.

Bad Dog

SECONDARY OBJECTIVE 6: CONTAIN ENEMY

TACMAP

Time is also of the essence. Some of the terrorists, realizing that they have been defeated, will attempt to escape via a small boat docked in an underground tunnel. You will have to eliminate all of the enemies down in the sub-level quickly, but carefully. There are most likely two more terrorists down at the bottom floor of the sub-level. Take the stairs slowly, with your sights trained on the doorway to the left. You should be able to pick them off as they come through before they ever even spot you.

PRIMARY OBJECTIVE 7: OBTAIN BIO AGENT

TACMAP

All that's left to do is locate and obtain Thong-kon's Bio Agent. It appears as though Thongkon was getting ready to pack it up and move on — you definitely arrived in the nick of time. The Agent is in a suitcase located at the end of the sub-level in the northeast corner of the room. Collect the containers and you have officially completed your mission.

CONGO: OPERATION SWIFT JUSTICE
MISSION 7: MERCENARY STAGING AREA

MISSION OVERVIEW:

"The Congolese government has requested our aid, team. A new mercenary organization calling themselves Preemptive Strike, has established a base of operations deep in the jungle. They are recruiting European strong-arms and are actively stockpiling weapons and ammunition. We are concerned about this new threat, but we need more information regarding their agenda and future plans. Infiltrate their camp, destroy targets of opportunity and gather as much Intel as possible."

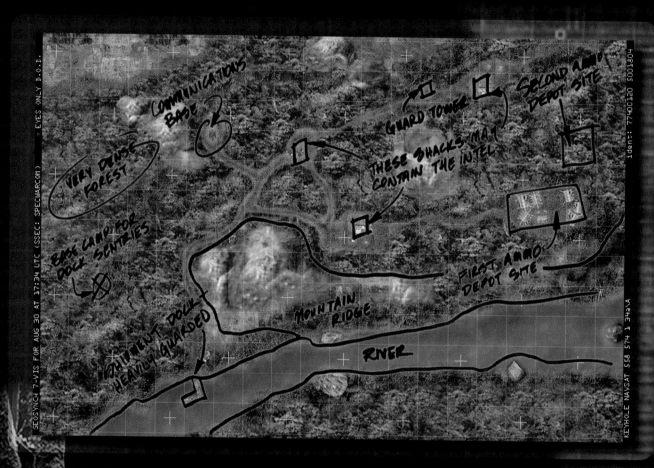

OBJECTIVES

PRIMARY OBJECTIVES

1. DISABLE COMMUNICATIONS
2. OBTAIN INTEL
3. DESTROY MUNITIONS
4. PREVENT ENEMY ESCAPE

SECONDARY OBJECTIVES

1. Secure Area
2. Site One Satchel
3. Site Two Satchel

PRIMARY OBJECTIVE 1: DISABLE COMMUNICATIONS

TACMAP

These mercenaries mean business. The little Intelligence that HQ has on Preemptive Strike shows that they are an extremely ruthless, violent and deadly group. Your best bet for accomplishing your mission is to remain unseen for as long as possible, using stealth kills and silenced weapons, until there is no other choice.

You can use the dense Congo jungle to your advantage, hiding in the tall grass, taking cover behind the large trees and generally sticking to the shadows whenever possible. Your first Primary Objective is to locate and disable the terrorists' Communication Tower before the mercs can radio for help and compromise the operation. The Communication Tower is due north at Nav Point Charlie, although you need to take a more stealthy route if you intend to get there without major incident.

There are two mercenaries directly in front of you to the west that require your immediate attention. If you try to take them out right away, you will most likely alert other guards in the area. Order Bravo to Hold Position, assume the Prone position and crawl into the thick brush. Slowly make your way through the foliage, staying out of their line of sight, and get as close as you can without alerting them to your presence.

Hang tight and watch them for a few minutes. After their brief conversation, they will separate and move out on patrol. The merc on the left will go in a westerly direction. The other will stay in the general area, either heading out onto the dock or patrolling around the crates littered about. A third might also appear, so be on the lookout before deciding to make your move.

When you feel confident that you can quietly eliminate the mercs from behind with stealth kills, or well-placed silenced shots, go to it. If their bodies are left out in the open, make sure you pick them up and move them out of the way into the brush or behind a tree.

CONTINGENCY PLAN

If you miss a shot or aren't able to kill a merc before they alert others in the area, you need to be prepared for a firefight. Many mercenaries will come running from a variety of different directions with their weapons trained on your position. Quickly order your Team to Fire at Will, as well as Regroup, and then find cover. You won't have the luxury of time for clean and accurate kills, as the mercs will head for the Tower to radio for help if given the chance. You need to take them out as quickly as possible and make for the Tower when you are confident that the immediate area is generally clear.

Stick around the insertion area and stay hidden for a few more moments. You need to make sure there are no other mercs patrolling the area or coming toward you. Eliminate any others you can find from your position quickly and quietly.

If you've been able to keep your position unknown, you can now begin to take care of the Preemptive Strike's Communications. Before heading out to the north toward the Communication Tower, there is a small camp off to the west that needs to be cleared. If you don't take care of the enemies inside it, they will attempt to ambush you or your team members later. Locate it on your TACMAP, and then carefully make your way in its direction, following the shore line to stay out of the enemy's line of sight and using the brush and trees for cover as you go.

There are a total of two more mercenaries guarding the small camp. Sneak around the back side and stealthfily make your way between the two tents, where you can eavesdrop on their conversation. As soon as they split up, or turn their backs to you, take them out with stealth kills.

You most likely will end up revealing your presence before you would like, so be prepared for action. As soon as you have eliminated the two in the camp, order Bravo to Regroup, and then Order Team to Fire at Will. Make your way north toward the Communication Tower, using the environment for cover, and pick off every mercenary you come across. Be sure to take a few seconds every so often to stop under the safety of relative cover and scan the area for any hostiles. With your SEAL team members' help, you should be able to eliminate each and every one without too much incident.

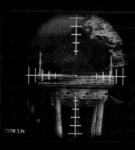

Be especially alert and careful around the guard towers, as they may or may not be occupied by mercs toting deadly M79 Grenade launching rifles. If you spot a merc up in a tower, try your best to pick them off from a safe distance. The first tower is just to the east, at the first branch of the dirt road.

The Communication Tower is located to the northeast, along the left branch of the dirt road. You will definitely encounter some resistance when you approach the Communications shack. Keep your eyes out for the area surrounding the shack and Tower, as multiple enemies will attack from all sides. Dig in and methodically take them out.

As soon as its clear, head inside the shack and shoot out the radio on the desk. Next, to completely cut off their communications, you'll need to go outside, point your cross hairs at the tower, and order Able to Deploy Satchel. Quickly leave the immediate area (you have approximately 10 seconds before it will detonate). The tower will explode, cutting off the mercs from the rest of their Preemptive Strike brothers.

PRIMARY OBJECTIVE 2: OBTAIN INTEL

TACMAP

The terrorists are holding a group of POWs somewhere deep in the Congo. Their whereabouts are unknown, but information HQ has gathered has revealed the mercs are keeping a Map with their location in a shack at Nav point Delta off to the east.

When you approach the shack, point your cross hairs in its general direction and order Bravo to Ambush. They will sweep the area for any hostiles, giving you a chance to infiltrate the shack and grab the Map sitting on the desk.

There also might be an enemy inside the shack, targeting you and your teammates through its window. Try to sneak around to the front door and, if it's closed, order Able or Bravo to Bang/Clear or Frag/Clear.

TACMAP

SECONDARY OBJECTIVE 1: SECURE AREA

 The area is literally crawling with enemies and, in order to complete your objectives, you and your SEAL team members need to eliminate and neutralize as many as possible. You will eventually need to make it all the way to Nav Point Juliet and destroy the enemy's Munitions Depot (which is due east) but, before heading that way, take the dirt road to the north (the left branch) and wipe out the mercs along its path. Order Bravo to Follow and head out.

  There is a second guard tower along the road, so watch out for the sniper inside it. While Bravo is keeping him busy, climb up the ladder and take him out with a stealth kill.

Finish up the sweep of the dirt road at the shack just beyond the tower. This is the route the enemy will use if they try to escape. By clearing it now, you will eliminate the possibility of anyone getting through after you destroy their supplies. If you go much farther past the shack, you will exit the area and prematurely finish your mission. Stop here, and turn your attention back toward Nav point Echo.

 As soon as you have taken out the enemies in this general area, head south toward Nav point Echo, keeping an eye out for any mercs along the way. If you come into contact with a group, order Bravo to Ambush and then help them out. There is another shack west of Echo where you'll find the cook. Leave no one standing.

When you've cleared the immediate area around Echo, it might look like you've completed your objective, but you will need to sweep the whole area between Echo and Juliet in order to accomplish it.

Enter the camp at Nav point Foxtrot carefully and eliminate the mercs guarding the first Weapons Depot. Be especially careful around the guard tower, as the merc above most likely has a grenade launcher. You will be attaching a Satchel to the stack of TNT crates in the middle of the camp, but only after you've cleared the entire area. Cautiously make your way toward Juliet. There is one final guard watching the second Depot, take him out and the area should be Cleared.

SECONDARY OBJECTIVE 2: SITE TWO SATCHEL

TACMAP

There are two Munitions Sites — one at Nav point Foxtrot (Site One) and the other at Juliet (Site Two). You need to place a Satchel Charge at each one to completely destroy their supplies. Since you are already at Foxtrot, the Depot at this location will be the first to go.

The first stack of TNT crates are situated at the foot of the hill at Nav point Juliet. Approach the crates and the "Place Satchel" icon will appear. Press the Action (✕) button to place it and head back toward Foxtrot.

SECONDARY OBJECTIVE 3: SITE ONE SATCHEL

TACMAP

The second stack of TNT crates are situated in the middle of the large wooden crates at Nav Point Foxtrot. Since you've used your only Satchel Charge, and you ordered Boomer to place his on the Communication Tower earlier, Bravo team is the only ones left with one in their Weapons Cache. Point your cross hairs over the TNT crates and order Bravo to Deploy Satchel. Objective completed.

PRIMARY OBJECTIVE 3: DESTROY MUNITIONS

TACMAP

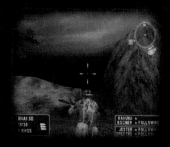

Now that both Satchels have been planted, you must move your team out of the blast area before they are detonated. The Satchels cannot be detonated until all members of your team are out of the blast area. With your team members following, head west and then north and make your way around the mountain toward the area you secured earlier. As soon as you get far enough away, Bravo will detonate the Satchels, destroying the Munitions in a fiery explosion.

PRIMARY OBJECTIVE 4: PREVENT ENEMY ESCAPE

TACMAP

The final objective is to restrain or eliminate all remaining mercenaries in the area. If they escape, they will warn their comrades that you are here, endangering the lives of the POWs. Make your way back to the dirt road to the north and scan its perimeter for any mercenaries. You might encounter a few trying to flee, so take them out before they can exit the area. You also might have completed this objective earlier, if you and your team members have neutralized all mercenaries in the area. Once done, your mission is accomplished. Great job!

MISSION 8: POW CAMP

MISSION OVERVIEW:

"You've eliminated some of the mercenaries, but there is always more scum. The remaining mercenaries have ambushed and captured a patrol of U.S. Marines. These marines are being held at the mercenary base camp where the merc's are torturing each one for Intel. They have already begun digging graves for the hapless soldiers. Infiltrate the area, eliminate any mercenary threats and protect the marines. Bring these men home, team."

OBJECTIVES

PRIMARY OBJECTIVES

1. INFILTRATE PERIMETER
2. SECURE ENTRY AREA
3. SECURE AREA TWO
4. SECURE POWS
5. CLEAR CAVES
6. EXTRACT POWS

SECONDARY OBJECTIVES

1. Eliminate Mercs
2. Recon Sentry
3. Verify POW Location

TACMAP

SECONDARY OBJECTIVE 1: ELIMINATE MERCS

The Preemptive Strike is holding the POWs somewhere deep in a jungle valley. Thanks to the map you acquired last mission, HQ was able to locate their camp. The camp itself is heavily guarded and there are many patrols and sentries stationed on and around its outlying border. The longer you can remain unseen, the better. If the camp leader, Magnus, suspects foul play, there's a chance the POWs won't survive. Your first order of business is to eliminate the mercs in and around the insertion area and then infiltrate the perimeter.

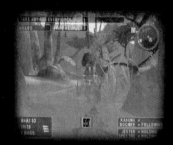

It won't be long until you encounter the first patrol. It's a good idea to stay off the trail and stick to the bush where you have a better chance at staying hidden and ambushing the enemy before they can react.
Order Bravo to Run to Charlie, which is located just a few yards from your insertion point, and then move yourself and Boomer into a hidden spot on the opposite side of the trail between the two large trees. Once there, order Bravo to Fire at Will. You should be able to catch the patrolling mercenaries in a crossfire, neutralizing them before they can alert any others.

There is another set of guards farther up the trail. Stick to the right side and use the dense foliage and large trees for cover as you slowly head south. When you get close enough, hang tight for a minute behind a tree until you are certain you will be able to quickly take them out. You could attempt to sneak up on one of them and execute a stealth kill while your team members eliminate the other, but it might be easier to pick them both off, one after the other, with your rifle.

PRIMARY OBJECTIVE 1: INFILTRATE PERIMETER

At your current position, you should be very close to the camp's perimeter. Hopefully, you've been able to eliminate the sentries without alerting any of the others to your presence. If you head up the trail a bit (staying to the side and under the cover of the environment), then you should be able to accomplish your Primary Objective without any other incident. Stay alert, though. This is just the beginning of a long and dangerous mission.

TACMAP

SECONDARY OBJECTIVE 2: RECON SENTRY

TACMAP

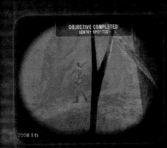

The mercenaries have posted sentries at the entry into the jungle valley at Nav point Delta. When you get to the opening along the trail, use your Binoculars or your M4A1 SD's scope to locate the sniper on the hill just off to your left. You can find the area on your TACMAP labeled "Lookout Point."

PRIMARY OBJECTIVE 2: SECURE ENTRY AREA

TACMAP

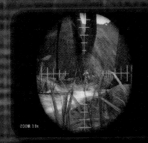

In order to successfully infiltrate the Mercenary Camp and rescue the POWs, you are going to have to do it bit by bit. Your next objective is to secure the entry area, which is located at Nav point Delta. Take out the sniper at Lookout Point and the other two mercs who will approach from the trail to the south. When they have been eliminated, you will have completed your Secondary Objective.

PRIMARY OBJECTIVE 3: SECURE AREA TWO

TACMAP

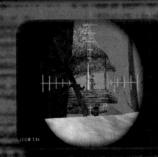

Area two is the southwestern section of the mercenary base. In order to maintain a stealth profile for as long as possible, it's best to totally deviate from the trail and follow the mountain wall to the right.

Keep an eye out for roaming patrols as you go, and definitely pay attention to the guard towers off in the distance. These towers generally have one or two snipers stationed inside, and they will spot you in an instant. You can use the high elevation to your advantage and pick them off with your rifle's scope.

Stay along the mountain wall to the right and come down into the misty valley. If you haven't already, order Bravo to Fire at Will, and then continue along the path displayed in your TACMAP. You will most certainly encounter plenty of enemies along the way. Use the large jungle trees for cover and pick them off quickly and as stealthfully as possible. When you get down to the bottom of the valley, your objective will be accomplished.

TACMAP

SECONDARY OBJECTIVE 3: VERIFY POW LOCATION

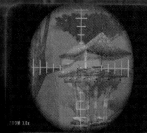

Continue along your current path, following the mountain wall to your right. There is a large over-hanging boulder just right of Nav point Echo that you can get up on and pick off a few mercenaries, both above and below. Watch your back while you're up here, as one or two might try to sneak up on you while you are concentrating on the enemy in the guard tower off in the distance.

According to the Map you found during your last mission, the POWs are located deep in the jungle, due south. There is a small mist-covered river that runs through the jungle just ahead, which should help keep you relatively hidden from enemy patrols.

When you've cleared the area of the temporary threat, climb back down and head into the river. Follow it, staying in the water, until you get to its end. You'll find a set of stone steps carved into the mountainside here that you can climb. These lead up to a vista point, overlooking the valley below. Again, use the mountain wall to your right as a guide and slowly make your way along its side toward the mercenary camp.

At one point, you'll ascend a hill around a large boulder. When you come around the other side, you will find yourself directly over the Mercenary Camp. Assume the Prone position so you'll be less likely to be seen and then Equip your Binoculars. If you scan the Camp, you should be able to spot a POW near the posts along the back fence. There is a second, being kept in a cell underneath the shack.

PRIMARY OBJECTIVE 4: SECURE POWS

TACMAP

There are actually three POWs being kept somewhere in the Camp, but only two are visible from your vantage point. You'll have to locate the third after you've saved and Secured the two below.

The Camp leader, Magnus, should also be somewhere in the immediate vicinity, and none too happy that you and your fellow SEAL team members are here. Stay in the prone position and engage him and any other mercenaries from where you are. Be careful not to hit the POWs, as their deaths result in complete mission failure.

When the camp is secure, move down and approach the POWs. The one by the posts tells you the other two POWs' names – Reilly and Beckman. Restrain him and then order him to Follow.

Head down into the cell to Restrain the second POW, Private William Joseph Beckman, who is a bit delirious from the torture he has endured. Order him to Follow as well.

From the limited information you've been able to gather from the two POWs, it sounds like the third is being held in the caves to the southeast. You won't be able to extract from the mission until you have all three, as well as have eliminated all of the hostiles from the area. Since the POWs are in no shape to fight, you are going to have to find a safe place for them to hide, until you can come back for them when it's safe. For the moment, keep them in Follow status and exit the Camp. You will not be able to complete this objective until you have found and Secured the final POW.

PRIMARY OBJECTIVE 5: CLEAR CAVES

TACMAP

Exit the camp and head due east, around the barbed wire fence and toward the Cave entrance with your team and POWs in tow. Don't let yourself get too far ahead of the POWs, as they are susceptible to enemy fire and make easy targets. Again, you want to use the mountain wall to your right as a guide. As you exit the Camp, you will find yourselves overlooking a small shack down to your left (located at Nav point Romeo). There are likely a few guards down below, so stay low and scan the area for any movement.

Follow the dirt path that leads down to the shack when you are confident that you have cleared the area below. Before heading inside and potentially endangering the lives of the POWs, point your cross hairs over the shack's door and order Able to Clear. He will kick open the door and make sure there are no hostiles waiting to ambush you inside.

When it's Clear, go inside. Make sure both of the POWs follow you in and, once they are both through the door, order them both to Hold Position. You are going to leave them inside the shack while you continue on your mission. They should be relatively safe for the time being. Make sure you close the door as you exit.

For added protection, point your cross hairs over the door and order Bravo to Cover Area. They will cover the shack and POWs for a while, allowing you to head toward the Cave entrance without worrying about the safety of the POWs. Try to leave at least one of them inside, if possible.

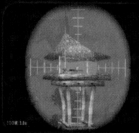

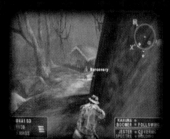

Continue east, following the path up along mountain wall, and make sure to watch out for any mercs patrolling the area. There is a second shack below (located at Nav point Whiskey) and another guard tower off in the distance to the left. Concentrate on the tower first, eliminating the two sentries inside and then turn your attention to the area around the shack. There are a handful of mercs surrounding the shack; be sure to pick them off from the safety of cover.

As before, order Able to Clear the shack, and then continue when the area is secure. The dirt path beyond the shack leads up to the Cave entrance. Go slow, keeping your eye out for any sentries coming from the entrance, and make your way up and inside.

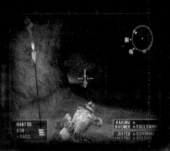
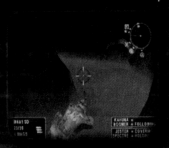

The Cave is actually a long tunnel running north through the mountain and coming out on the other side. There are two alcoves inside where the third and final POW could be held. Since the cave tunnel is fairly straight, with very little corners, obstructions or curves, there aren't many opportunities for cover. Stick as close to the walls as possible and peek around corners whenever you can.

You will eventually come to an opening in the tunnel, which branches out into the two alcoves. Use the large boulders along the wall to your right for cover and try to spot any mercenaries inside. It's a good idea to listen as well as look, as these mercenaries are not the smartest terrorists around, and will shout and holler as they are coming for you, letting you know which direction they are coming from, and how many of them there are. Pick them off as they come running for you. At this point, it's entirely possible you've completed your objective and Cleared the Caves.

Head up into the right alcove first. It should be empty (unless the merc didn't come out to attack you). When you've verified that there is no one inside, go back down and move up into the one to the left.

You'll find the third POW inside, who is in shock and can't remember his name. He'll have plenty of time to rest and rehabilitate later, Restrain him and order him to Follow, completing your objective.

Now that all POWs have been located and secured, you need to exit the Cave and secure the entry area, then get all three to the extraction point at Nav point Zulu. It's possible Bravo is no longer in a Covering position. If this is the case, order them to Hold Position, so they will stay in the general vicinity of the POWs. Continue through the Cave, with POW in tow, until you get to the exit on the other end. You might now encounter more hostiles along the way, and you also won't have completed the Primary Objective. You'll have to go back and perform another sweep, once you've moved the third POW into a safe place.

Back outside, follow the dirt path and cross the small wood bridge at Nav point Foxtrot. Be aware of the guard tower off in the distance to your right. There is a sniper stationed inside. On the other side of the bridge, you will find a camp. Hopefully, it's deserted, but there might be one or two lingering mercs around its perimeter. Carefully sweep the area and eliminate any hostiles you encounter.

Refer to your TACMAP and locate the shack where you have left the other two POWs and head over to it. Bravo should still be in the general area, but you might encounter a few patrolling mercs in its vicinity. Quickly take them out before they have a chance to shoot the POWs inside.

CAVE CONTINGENCY PLAN

If you haven't accomplished the objective of Clearing the Caves, you will have to go back for a second sweep. When it's safe, head back inside the shack and order the third POW to Hold Position. Once again, close the door behind you and order Bravo to Cover Area while you head back into the Cave with Boomer and perform a second sweep.

You'll definitely encounter a few more patrolling mercs, both outside the entrance and inside its tunnels. By the time you get to the exit, you should have Cleared the Cave and completed your Primary Objective. Now all that's left to do is to grab the POWs and deliver them safely to the extraction point at Nav point Zulu.

PRIMARY OBJECTIVE 6: EXTRACT POWS

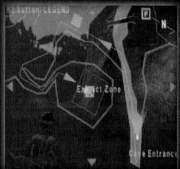

By now, you should be very familiar with the location of the shack where you've left the POWs. It's just across the bridge and due south at Nav point Roger. Head back over there and order all three of them individually to Follow. Don't forget to also order Bravo to Follow as well.

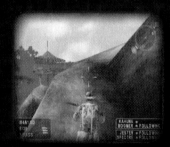

The extraction point is located atop a small hill to the north, just above the camp and bridge near the Cave exit. There is a dirt trail that leads up to the hill which, in turn, has a path that leads up to the extraction point. It's possible that you will encounter some resistance along the way, although it's unlikely. Be careful in any case and make your way there slowly and deliberately. It would be a travesty to lose a man so close to completing your mission. When all three POWs make it up the hill to the extraction point, it's mission accomplished.

MISSION 9: MOUNTAIN ASSAULT

MISSION OVERVIEW:

"One captive Marine was not in the river camp. The mercenaries relocated him before your arrival. They will not be able to move him again. We've isolated the Marine's current location and you're going to save him, SEAL Team. Infiltrate this mercenary stronghold in the Congolese jungle. You are authorized to use any force necessary to return the Marine alive. Good luck, team."

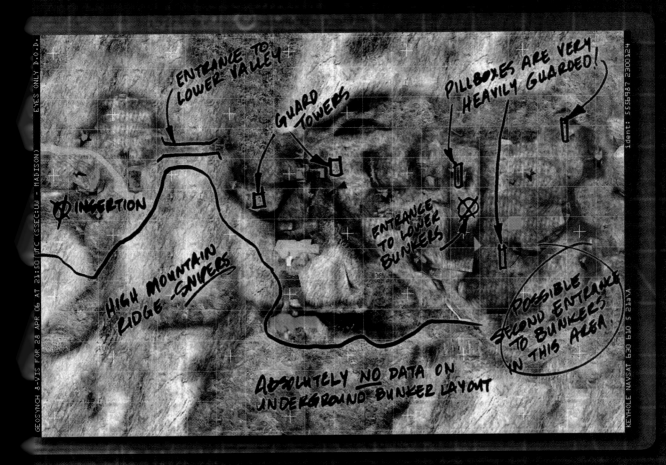

OBJECTIVES

PRIMARY OBJECTIVES

1. CLEAR TOWERS
2. AIR STRIKE BUNKER 1
3. AIR STRIKE BUNKER 2
4. AIR STRIKE BUNKER 3
5. INFILTRATE BUNKER
6. DISABLE FUSEBOX
7. SECURE MARINE

SECONDARY OBJECTIVES

1. Disable Battery

R2 button: LEGEND

TACMAP

PRIMARY OBJECTIVE 1: CLEAR TOWERS

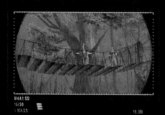

Preemptive Strike is on the run. Their last refuge is an abandoned German Bunker, which was created during World War I and used as a network of underground tunnels and pillboxes. Its main entrance is barred shut and impenetrable from your arsenal of explosives, making a frontal assault next to impossible. Infrared surveillance has found a possible second entrance into the Bunker, which is located somewhere off to the north. Along the way, you are going to have to Clear the two guard towers and have support Air Strike a trio of Pillboxes.

As soon as you insert into the mission, you'll encounter two mercenaries atop a bridge, as well as a patrol making their rounds directly underneath. Use the thick brush for cover, assume the Prone position, equip your Nightvision Goggles, and wait for them to come into view. As soon as you see the three mercs patrolling below, Order Team to Ambush and then help out and eliminate the group of hostiles as quickly as possible.

When you have neutralized the immediate threat, order Bravo to Follow and go southwest, across the small stream to the left. Follow the stream up and then go around the large tree and rock formation, so you're heading north, back toward the bridge. As you move around the rock formation, you might come across two more mercs, who have their backs toward you. Try to kill them stealthily, if possible, taking them out quickly and silently.

Just off to your left, down the long sloping path, there is a second, small group of mercs. They have blockades set up, protecting them from hostile fire. Make sure your cross hairs are pointed in their general direction and Order Team to Ambush once again.

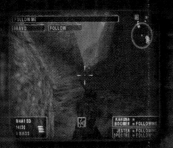 

 When the dust has settled, order Bravo to Follow, and carefully make your way down the sloping path. Around the corner at its end, you should be able to peek out and pick off a few more guards off in the distance. You should also be able to spot the first Tower, which is to the northeast.

Quickly leave Bravo behind and run up the hill to the Tower. Hopefully, the sniper above will be busy trying to target your teammates, while you Climb the ladder and take him out with a Rifle Butt to the head. That's one down and one to go.

 Head back down the small hill the Tower is located on and then continue northeast down the path. You'll pass by a majestic waterfall along the path, although there is no time to stop and admire its beauty. Continue down the path, using the bushes, grass and environment for cover and protection as you descend.

If you find yourself coming across a patrol of mercs, quickly take cover and pick them off methodically. Make sure you Order Team to Fire at Will, so they won't hesitate to join in the battles.

  When you get to the bottom of the sloping path, it will start to ascend. The second Tower is up the path a bit off to the right. Head up the path to the right and order Bravo to Cover the path, which leads out into a valley, while you head for the Tower above. Again, climb the ladder up to the Tower and quickly take out the sniper inside before he has a chance to react to your presence. Objective complete.

PRIMARY OBJECTIVE 2: AIR STRIKE BUNKER 1

TACMAP

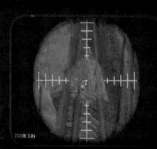

Slide down the ladder, and rejoin your SEAL team members on the path below. Order them to Follow, then continue along the right path and carefully head around the bend. Your next Nav point is Foxtrot, which is off to the north. Go slowly, and continue to use the environment for cover. You will continue to encounter resistance as you move forward.

You should come to a branch in the path. Take a moment to scan the area and see if you can locate any mercenaries ahead. There should be at least one up on a rock off to the left. Get in the brush and pick him off before he can get a visual on you.

The first Bunker is just past Nav point Foxtrot off to the north. As you approach Foxtrot, you'll find the main entrance to the underground Bunker. Don't even bother trying to blow it open with an explosive, the door is impenetrable. You'll have to try to find that second entrance HQ referred to.

There is a set of two large trees in front and to the left of the main entrance. Position yourself against the trees, facing toward the path and main entrance to the Bunker. Order Bravo to Cover Area, and they will protect you, allowing you to concentrate on Lasing Bunker 1, which is just beyond the trees in the opposite direction.

Next, hug the tree and peek out so you are facing Bunker 1, which is up on a ridge to the north. The Bunker is heavily armored and you can't climb up there (which you wouldn't want to anyway). There are also snipers inside, making it virtually impregnable to an assault. The only way you are taking it out is to order an Air Strike from above.

LASING AND AIR STRIKES

In missions where you need to order an Air Strike on a specific target, you will be equipped with a Laser Designator as your secondary weapon. When you find and locate your target, equip your Laser Designator and point your cross hairs over it. When you are ready to lase your target, hold down the Fire (R1) button, which will activate the Designator and give air support a target from above. Lasing a target takes a total of 15 seconds to execute, and if you stop in the middle of lasing, you will need to start over from scratch. Be careful when you lase a target, as it is a perfect time for an enemy to ambush you.

Equip your secondary weapon, which is a Laser Designator. Point your cross hairs at the Bunker above, using the large tree for cover from the sniper fire, and lase the target. It will take approximately 15 seconds for air support to lock on to the target, but Bravo will be watching your back, giving you the breathing room you need to get it done. As soon as the meter in the right side of your screen fills, you will see the target taken out from a missile above.

PRIMARY OBJECTIVE 3: AIRSTRIKE BUNKER 2

TACMAP

Now that you have taken out the first of three Bunkers, you need to finish off the other two. According to your TAC-MAP, Bunker 2 is off to the east. Make sure your team is ordered to Follow and head off in that direction. You'll have to backtrack toward Foxtrot and then take the right branch in the path to get there.

Follow the path and continue to watch out for patrolling mercenaries. HQ will contact you along the way and give you more details on the hidden entrance to the underground Bunker. According to their Intelligence, it's located somewhere around Nav point Zulu. You'll be heading there in a bit but, first, you still have two more Bunkers to lase.

Bunker 2 is at the top of the path, off in the distance to the left. You should be able to see the Bunker from a vantage point between a large rock outcropping on the left side and a large tree on the right. Take a few seconds to sweep the area directly below this vantage point before attempting to lase the Bunker, as there are patrolling mercs below. You can also order Bravo to Cover Area here, as well.

When all is clear, equip and aim your Designator at the Bunker (using the tree to the right for cover) and lase it. 15 seconds later, Bunker 2 will be destroyed.

TACMAP

PRIMARY OBJECTIVE 4: AIRSTRIKE BUNKER 3

The dirt path continues up and off to the left. Use the foliage along the way for cover, picking off any mercs you might encounter, and head toward the west. You'll eventually get Bunker 3 in your sights. Stop at the tall grass, use it for cover and lase the third and final Bunker (which is just beyond the grass). Your Primary Objective should now be complete.

TACMAP

PRIMARY OBJECTIVE 5: INFILTRATE BUNKER

Refer to your TACMAP for the secret entrance to the Bunker complex. It is east of your location, very close to Nav point Zulu. Head in that direction, using the mountain wall to your left as a guide to lead you to it. Make sure to listen and look for any patrols along the way, eliminating them as you go. You'll most likely encounter a set right in front of the entrance. Before going inside the entrance, toss an M67 Grenade into the doorway, killing any lingering mercs inside. When it's all clear, enter the Bunker and make your way down into its interior.

SECONDARY OBJECTIVE: DISABLE BATTERY

TACMAP

Disable the battery that provides emergency power.

The ramp inside the Bunker leads down into a network of tunnels. If you can locate the Bunker's Fusebox, you will be able to disable the power inside, unlocking the cell door to where they are keeping the final POW hostage. In order to keep the power from being reactivated, you will also need to disable three reserve Batteries, which are located in different locations.

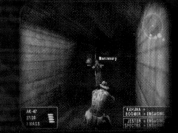

 Follow the tunnel down into the complex. It leads into a room guarded by a mercenary. If you're quick enough, you can pick him off before he can return fire. You can also shoot out the lights along the tunnel ceiling and equip your Nightvision Goggles, making it difficult for the terrorists to see while giving you the upper hand.

The next room you come to branches off with a ramp leading down to a lower level to your left, and a second tunnel that continues off to the south. Leave the ramp for the time being, and continue through the next room and into the next tunnel. Be prepared for anything, including ambushing mercenaries around each corner.

You'll find a darkened room around the first corner, which houses the first Battery in the right corner of the room. Listen for the hum of electricity to aid you in the darkness if you are having trouble locating it. Switch it off by pressing the Action (✗) button when the "Battery Off" switch appears.

The second Battery is down at the end of the tunnel, in a small closet-sized room to the right. Be careful, as there might be a merc in the left room on the opposite side of the tunnel. Switch it off and then get ready to move on. For reference, the set of doors at the end of the tunnel are the main doors you weren't able to get through outside.

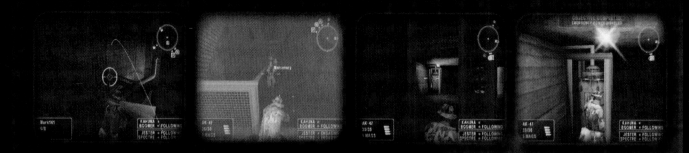

The third and final Battery is located on the lower level of the Bunker. Make your way back to the room with the ramp and, before heading down, equip your Mark 141 Stun Grenade then toss it over to the lower level. There are two mercs directly below, and you should be able to stun them and then eliminate them in a blink of an eye. When you get to the bottom of the ramp, you'll find the third Battery in the room to the left. Flip the switch, and you will have disabled them all.

TACMAP

PRIMARY OBJECTIVE 6: DISABLE FUSEBOX

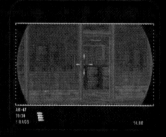

The Fusebox is located in a small room down at the end of the corridor, set in the wall. Equip your Nightvision Goggles and move very cautiously. The tight spaces, stacked crates and blind corners down here make you and your SEAL team members easy targets. When you enter the room, listen for any enemies inside — it's possible they will lose their cool and betray their hiding spaces. There is most likely one merc hiding behind a crate tucked into the left corner of the room, and another behind the set that are in front of the small hallway leading to the Fusebox.

When the threat has been eliminated, Open the Door to the Fusebox and then Cut the Wires inside. Once accomplished, the metallic lock holding the final Marine is now unlocked. All that's left to do is to Secure him for extraction.

PRIMARY OBJECTIVE 7: SECURE MARINE

TACMAP

The final POW is being held in a cell in the southern-most room in the Bunker. Now that you have disabled the Fusebox, the door blocking your way should be unlocked. It's just to the left inside the same room with the Fusebox.

Don't head in until you've ordered your Team to Bang /Clear. There are at least two mercenaries guarding the Marine inside. Use the confusion of the Flash Grenade to quickly eliminate them. When it's safe to do so, Restrain the final POW. As soon as he's secure, victory is yours. Another successful mission has been completed.

TURKMENISTAN: OPERATION SERPENT STRIKE
MISSION 10: PRISON BREAK

MISSION OVERVIEW:

"We have a new mission for you, team. One of our indigenous informants in Turkmenistan, Basim Maccek (a.k.a. Mr. Pickle), went silent last week. This week we know why. He is imprisoned in a Turkmen Detention Center in the mountains. We suspect that Maccek's learned something about portable nuclear devices rumored to be on the move through the Middle East. You've got to get Maccek, SEALs. Find out what he knows and escort him to safety."

OBJECTIVES

PRIMARY OBJECTIVES

1. INFILTRATE PRISON
2. RELEASE INFORMANT
3. ACQUIRE MAP
4. EXTRACT INFORMANT

SECONDARY OBJECTIVES

1. Explosive Diversion
2. Disable Generator
3. Secure Informant

PRIMARY OBJECTIVE 1: INFILTRATE PRISON

It's critical you infiltrate the Prison and rescue Pickle. The Prison, a dilapidated former Soviet Detention Center in the mountains south of the Capital City of Ashgabat, is heavily guarded both inside and out. In order to infiltrate it successfully (and with minimal damage and casualties), stealth and diversionary tactics are the only way to go. To accomplish this mission objective with the least amount of resistance, you also should fulfill Secondary Objective 1: Explosive Diversion.

According to Intelligence gathered, you have a total of 15 minutes to get in and out of the Prison before the enemy's patrolling Hind Helicopter returns. Make every second count.

The Prison entrance is off in the distance, across a bridge to the north, but you won't get very far knocking on their front door. The only way in is over the back wall. Silent kills are the only way you will be able to achieve your objectives. From your insertion point, take a right and slowly move around the large boulder. If you peek out around its side, you will spot two stationary guards. Wait until you are confident that their backs are facing you and you can eliminate them both quickly, without letting them get a shot off. It's best to pick them off from afar with your rifle rather than trying to execute a stealth kill.

Deviate from the sandy tire tracks and follow the mountain wall to the right. You can stay in its shadow by hugging its side, making it harder for the enemy to spot you. There is a path at the end that leads down into a canyon. You can bet that there is at least one guard patrolling its perimeter. Go slow, and use the large rock and shadows to your advantage. You should be able to take the lone sentry by surprise. Make sure you are using your silenced M4A1 SD rifle or stealth kills on the unsuspecting enemy. Also, only shoot if you have a clean shot. You don't want to let your enemy alert others with his gunfire or screams for help. If given the chance, all enemies will bolt for the Prison entrance and sound the alarm. You don't want to let that happen.

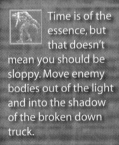

Time is of the essence, but that doesn't mean you should be sloppy. Move enemy bodies out of the light and into the shadow of the broken down truck.

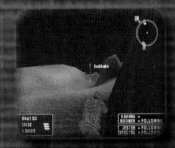

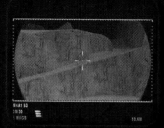

When it looks relatively safe, scan the area across the canyon and along the path carved into the mountainside with your Nightvision Goggles and see if you can locate any other potential threats. If you do locate an enemy, wait and watch to see where his patrol takes him. You don't want to shoot a terrorist who might be near the Prison entrance above, as there are probably a few more patrolling the immediate area. They will notice his dead body and sound the alarm if given the chance.

You can, however, safely take out any enemies down in the canyon or across the way along the path leading back up the other side -- as long as you have a clean shot.

When you get to the bottom of the canyon, stick to the shadows and use the large boulders in the sand for visual cover. Cross the span of the canyon silently and head up the path on the other side.

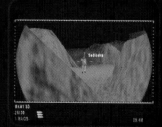
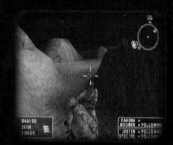

When you get up on the other side of the canyon, use the dark shadows for cover and take a few moments to scan the area with your Nightvision Goggles. Look for enemy movement in the immediate area and eliminate the threat. Remember, not to shoot any terrorists in front of the Prison.

You also don't want to leave any alive along the right wall of the Prison. They will bolt for the entrance and alarm if you are spotted.

Continue to use the right side of the mountain wall as your guide and for cover. The shadows it throws on the sandy ground should provide enough camouflage to keep you hidden from the guard towers inside the Prison walls.

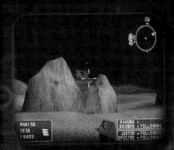 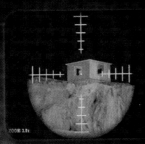  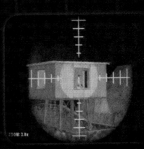

Speaking of guard towers, there are three of them along the Prison's walls -- two along the east side and one against the back (refer to your TACMAP to get their exact locations.) Using your rifle's scope, you should be able to locate and pick off the guard inside the first one when he moves in front of the window. Be patient and wait until you are sure you have a clean head shot before taking out the target.

Continue following the mountain wall, scanning the area for any patrolling sentries, until you have the second guard tower in your sights. Get close enough that you are sure you can do some damage and, once again, acquire and pick off the target inside.

  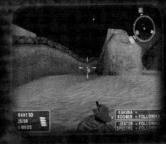 

By now, you should have made it to the back side of the Prison walls. If you have used stealth, you should not have triggered any alarms and have not alerted the terrorists to your presence. If you have blown your cover, you still can infiltrate the Prison, you just won't have the element of surprise and the odds will be much less favorable. There is a small boulder in the sand along the back wall at Nav point Delta with which you can use to climb up and over the wall. If the enemy is aware of you, quickly head over to it and climb up and over the wall.

If you are still undetected, continue using the mountain wall as your guide and for cover, moving slowly, watching out for any patrolling guards. You should encounter at least one along the back side.

There is a path to your right that leads north between the mountains along the back wall. This will be the path you take when you have secured Pickle for extraction. For now, follow the Prison wall as it turns a corner to the left. Remember to use the large boulders and any other obstructions for cover.

Continue following the Prison wall -- it will lead you to Nav point Charlie. That loud sound you are probably hearing is most likely the Generator, which will need to be disabled for you to successfully accomplish your mission. You won't be taking care of it for a few more minutes, as it is located inside the Prison walls.

Be very careful of the third guard tower when you get to the back portion of the Prison wall. It is easy to miss along the way, and the sentry inside has a clear view of the perimeter from his vantage point. Use the large boulder in the sand for cover and wait for him to appear in the window. When you have a clean shot, eliminate him.

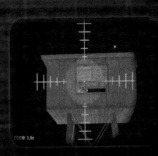

TACMAP

TACMAP

SECONDARY OBJECTIVE 1: EXPLOSIVE DIVERSION

Eventually, you will come to Nav point Charlie and the portion of wall that is cracked with decay. A well-placed Satchel Charge will create enough of a diversion here, enabling you and your fellow SEAL team members to sneak inside by climbing over the wall back at Nav point Delta. Move up to the wall and place a Satchel Charge when the Satchel Charge icon appears.

You have approximately 25 seconds to make your way back to Nav point Delta before the Charge blows. When you arrive, make sure you don't climb over the wall until the Charge has been detonated. Doing so prematurely will result in exposing your presence to the enemy. Your team might be assaulted by a sniper on a roof along the way. Try to pick him off if you get the chance. When the Charge explodes, the terrorists inside the Prison will head over to the area to check it out. It's time to move!

To finish your Primary Objective of infiltrating the Prison, climb over the Prison wall at Nav point Delta using the small boulder set in the ground against it, and then drop down inside.

SECONDARY OBJECTIVE 2: DISABLE GENERATOR

Even though you've created a diversion, there will still be a few guards who have remained at their posts. As soon as you drop down inside the Prison, they will most likely be aware of your presence. Quickly order your Team to Fire at Will, assess the threat in the immediate area, take out any hostiles you can, and then make way for the Generator, which is just to your right.

There are two ways you can take out the Generator. The first is by approaching it and disabling it by hand, when the Disable Generator icon appears. This is a lengthy process, taking approximately 10 seconds to achieve and leaving you painfully exposed to enemy fire.

The second and less elegant (but much safer) method is to toss a Grenade at it (or attach C-4 to it -- if you have it in your Weapons Cache). As long as the Grenade lands in close proximity to the Generator, it will be completely destroyed. Whichever way you choose, once carried out, your objective will be completed.

PRIMARY OBJECTIVE 2: RELEASE INFORMANT

TACMAP

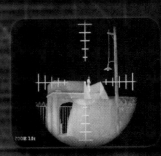

From the Intel HQ has gathered, Pickle is being held in a Cell Block along the east side of the Prison. Locate it on your TACMAP and then cautiously make your way over to it. Use the structures and boulders along the way for cover and, before going in, take a moment or two to eliminate any hostiles you can find. There should be quite a few clustered in and around the front entrance of the Prison, as well as a few that might try to ambush you from behind the Cell Block in the opposite direction. Stay put and under cover until you are sure that you have eliminated as many as possible. Be aware that these terrorists have no problem liberally tossing grenades your way. Watch for smoking projectiles and run if you see one heading in your direction.

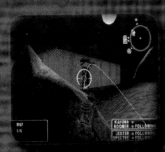

When the immediate threat has been quelled, move close to the Cell Block but don't go in. There are likely one or two guards just inside the doorway waiting to ambush you and your team. Instead, throw an M67 Frag Grenade through the door to even the odds.
As soon as the smoke clears, you can either order your Team to Clear, or you can peek in and pick off any survivors.

As soon as you and your team are inside, take precautionary measures by turning around and pointing your cross hairs over the open doorway. Order Team to Cover Area, and they will take out any hostiles that attempt to come in while you are searching for your man.

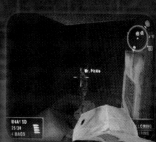

The Cell Block is a makeshift jail with three holding cells on either side. Mr. Pickle is located inside one of these cells. The cells hold four prisoners including Pickle, but he's the only one you want. He could be in any one of the cells, so you will have to search them all. As per protocol, Restrain the prisoners as you go along and, when you find Pickle, Restrain him as well.

TACMAP

SECONDARY OBJECTIVE 3: SECURE INFORMANT

Apparently, the terrorists have taken Pickle's Map and stashed it away inside the Armory. Before you can acquire it, you need to Secure Pickle in a safe place and have Bravo team guard him. The safest building is the one smack dab in the middle of the Prison. Locate it on your TAC-MAP and prepare to head out.

Order Pickle to Follow, as well as order your Team to Follow, and then cautiously exit the Cell Block. The safe house is just west of the Cell Block, off to the right.

You have very limited time before the Hind returns from its patrol. If you fall in its sights, you will most likely not survive. Head out of the Cell Block with Mr. Pickle in tow, and then make a run for the main building. It is just to the right of the Cell Block and the door is on the south side.

Head inside and move into the second room (there is a set of lockers against one of the walls). When Pickle is inside, he will be safely Secured for the moment.

Order Pickle to Hold Position, and then point your cross hairs over him and order Bravo to Cover Area, leaving them to ensure his safety while you head out to the Armory to recover his map.

PRIMARY OBJECTIVE 3: ACQUIRE MAP

TACMAP

According to HQ, they have located the enemy Hind, which is heading your way and will be at your location in less than a minute. There's no time to lose. Leave Pickle in Bravo's capable hands and head out toward the Armory, which is located behind the main building to the west. Make sure you locate it on your TACMAP before heading over to it. You don't want to make any mistakes that might cost you precious seconds.

Outside, be on the lookout for any hostiles, especially snipers on rooftops. Again, use the rocky terrain for cover and quickly pick them off if you spot any.

The Armory is the last building to the west, up on the hill. There are multiple entrances you can use, but the best one is around the back by the far wall. Be careful as you enter, as there are most likely hostiles inside.

The Map you're looking for is in one of two places. The first place is on a desk on the first floor in the second room, which is just beyond the closed door. The second place is upstairs. You'll find it resting on a second desk above. With either location, move carefully through the Armory, as there are multiple guards lurking about inside. Find and grab the Map, and the Secondary Objective is now complete.

TACMAP

PRIMARY OBJECTIVE 4: EXTRACT INFORMANT

You need to move Mr. Pickle to the extraction zone, which is located northwest of the Prison, outside its walls, past Nav point Foxtrot. Unfortunately, the enemy Hind is either on its way back to the Prison or has already returned, and it will make quick work of you, Pickle and your fellow SEAL team members if you are caught out in the open.

TAKING DOWN THE HIND

The Hind Helicopter is old and unsound, making destroying it a much more realistic possibility. Hightail it back to the building where you left Pickle and Bravo. Leave Bravo Covering Pickle for the moment, and position yourself so you are just inside the building, right in front of the doorway. From this position, you can use the corrugated awning over the doorway as cover, and then peek out and fire a few rounds at the Hind when you get it in your sights. Make sure your rifle is set for maximum burst and your Nightvision Goggles are equipped. As soon as you feel vulnerable, or take a hit from its spray of bullets, duck back inside the building for cover and temporary reprieve. You are going to have to repeat the process numerous times, but eventually you will succeed in taking the Helo down.

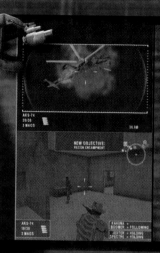

As soon as you have brought down the Hind, you will be presented with a new objective to Recon the Enemy Encampment. You'll be dealing with this objective momentarily, but you still have to get out of the Prison alive. Order Pickle and Bravo to Follow, and then move out. There are two ways out of the Prison, either through the front gate, which you can open by pulling the lever on the left side of the gate, or through the hole in the Prison wall, which you created during your diversion. The hole is the best way to go, as the extraction route at Nav point Foxtrot is much closer and quicker this way.

If you didn't blow the hole in the wall earlier, you will have to use the front entrance. Just beware of any hostiles who still might be lurking on the other side of the gate.

Lead Pickle and Bravo out of the Prison and toward Foxtrot. You probably won't encounter any resistance along the way, although you should still tread very carefully and also make sure that you don't get too far ahead of them. Make sure you frequently turn around and stop, letting them catch up. When you get to Foxtrot, head down the pathway between the two mountains you spotted earlier. This route will take you down to the extraction zone a few hundred yards past Nav Point Foxtrot.

SECONDARY OBJECTIVE 4: RECON ENCAMPMENT

TACMAP

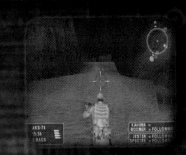

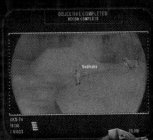

  Unfortunately, before you can extract from the mission, you will first need to observe and then eliminate the terrorist troops in the Encampment ahead. As you round the corner toward Nav point Foxtrot, you'll see a small ledge dead ahead along the left mountain wall.
Stop short of the ledge and order Pickle to Hold Position, then point your cross hairs in his general direction and order Bravo to Attack to Cross Hairs. Bravo will guard him, attacking and eliminating any enemies that might attempt to take him out. Next, leave them behind and climb up to the ridge. There is a cluster of grass up here which you can use as cover. Slowly crouch walk up to it and make sure you are hidden from view by any enemies below. Equip your Nightvision Goggles and then scan the area below. You should be able to spot at least three hostiles down in the Encampment. Once you have gotten all of them in your sights, you will have completed the objective.

As long as you are up on the ridge, use the high vantage point to your advantage. Take out as many of the enemy as you can find below, which should end up being at least six or seven. When you feel the immediate threat has been quelled, return to Pickle and Bravo and order them to Follow.
Go slow and move cautiously through the Enemy Encampment. You'll likely encounter a few more resisting terrorists as you make your way to the Extraction zone. Be sure to eliminate them quickly, as you wouldn't want to lose Pickle, so close to the end.

There is one final enemy up on the bridge just in front of the Extraction zone. He is particularly tough to target and will try to take out Pickle if given the chance. Do your best to neutralize him, using whatever means available.

Move just a little further down the path and under the bridge, and you will have made it in one piece to the Extraction zone. Mission accomplished. Great job, SEALs.

111

TURKMENISTAN: OPERATION SERPENT STRIKE
MISSION 11: MOUTH OF THE BEAST

MISSION OVERVIEW:

"Good work recovering our informant. He has confirmed the presence of at least two suitcase Nukes in Turkmenistan and his map will help you with our new problem. The men holding Maccek were members of a terrorist organization, the Allah Sadikahu. We know their leader, Mullah Bahir Al-Qadi. His reputation as a ruthless commander is well known. The Sadikahu have concealed their portable nuclear devices in a desert cave network close to the Afghan border. Locate and destroy the Nukes. We believe Al-Qadi is also at this location. If found, he is to be neutralized. Eliminate all other hostile threats. Show them what we're made of Team."

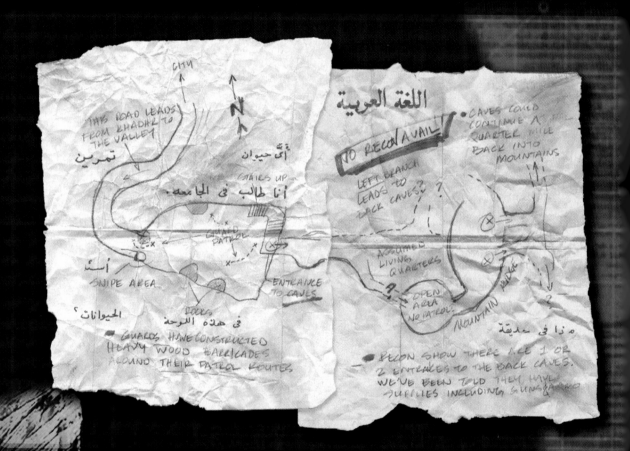

OBJECTIVES

PRIMARY OBJECTIVES

1. INSERT INTO CAVES
2. LOCATE VAULT
3. SECURE NUKES
4. DISARM NUKE
5. RESET NUKE
6. MOVE TO EXTRACTION

SECONDARY OBJECTIVES

1. Disable Radio Comm
2. Disable Generator

SECONDARY OBJECTIVE 1: DISABLE RADIO COMM

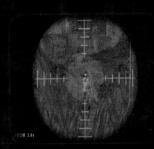

TACMAP

The Sadikahu are keeping the Nukes somewhere deep inside a network of Caves near the Afghan border. Your mission is to infiltrate the Caves and Secure the Nukes at all costs. From the limited Intel available, HQ has been able to determine that the terrorists are communicating through Radio Comm units. If they are able to radio back to Al-Qadi, who is believed to be somewhere inside, your mission will be highly compromised. The last thing you want to do is let them know you're here too early. Stealth is of the utmost importance for as long as possible.

The Radio Comm unit is behind a makeshift shelter east of your insertion point at Nav point Delta. Getting to it undetected won't be easy, but that's why you're the best of the best. Use the rocky terrain and tall grass around the corner for cover and locate the first of many enemies in the immediate area. He should be in the general vicinity, either on the left or right hand side of the canyon walls. As soon as you have a bead on him, take him out silently with a head shot.

Quickly head over to the left side of the canyon wall and inch forward until you get to the covered corner. There is another guard patrolling the immediate area, but you don't want to eliminate him until you recon the rest of the area.

Stay in the crouched position and use the brush here to slowly edge around the corner to the left. Stay inside the foliage and keep down until you come around the corner. From this vantage point, you should be able to spot a third terrorist, who is holding his post just beyond a broken down fence. Make him your next target and take him out only when you are sure you have a clean head shot.

There are definitely more guards in the immediate area. If you reveal yourself, they will make a dash for the Radio Comm and alert the others inside to your presence. Take a moment to pinpoint your next target, which should be somewhere around your 2:00 (if you are facing the fence). Pick him off. There should be another guard making his rounds somewhere along the right region of the canyon. Swivel around and scan the area, but be sure to stay in the cover of the brush. When you spot him, confirm that there are no others in visual range and take him out. If you can't find him, or any others, then it's time to move on.

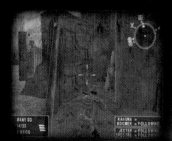

Stay put for another moment and make sure there is no other movement in the area. If you can get a visual on any other targets, take them out. When you feel it is safe to do so, head out of your cover and make a dash for the large boulder in the middle of the canyon.

Edge around it to the right, using its bulk for cover as you go, and then take another moment to scan the area. Directly ahead, you should see a series of makeshift shelters that could possibly hide more enemies, as well as the Radio unit.

Cautiously head over to the shelters, and slip behind them. To the left is the Radio Comm. There are two ways to Disable it. You can either switch it off by approaching it and pressing the Action (✕) button when the "Comm Unit" icon appears, or by shooting it. At this point, you should definitely switch it off manually, as the sound of your gunfire destroying it might alert others.

SEAL PRESENCE REVEALED: CONTINGENCY PLAN

If you mistakenly reveal your presence before you can eliminate all of the hostiles in the area, quickly order Team to Fire at Will and then make a dash for the Radio Comm, which is located at the base of the Cave's stairs, behind a makeshift shelter at Nav point Delta. Try to eliminate any hostiles as you go, and be careful of any terrorists hiding behind the shelters near the Radio. As soon as you spot it, take it out with a well-placed shot.

TACMAP

PRIMARY OBJECTIVE 1: INSERT INTO CAVES

The Cave entrance is located above, at the top of the stairs. You can access the stairs on the northern-most side of the canyon. Stay low and use the rocky terrain for cover as you slowly move in that direction. When you get to the stairs, use the small stair wall on your right for cover and peek around the corner at the landing.

If you don't spot any guards at the top of the stairs, make a dash up the next set and over to the left wall. There is a Generator here, along with the left wall, which you can use for cover.

GENERATORS

The Sadikahu draw electricity from a series of run-down Generators placed throughout the Cave network. These Generators are used to power the lights, as well as the Radio units inside. By Disabling these units, you will be able to take out the lights, giving you a tactical advantage with your Nightvision Goggles. You can flip a switch to disable them, or use an explosive device, such as a Grenade or C-4. Since you don't want to alert the enemy to your presence for as long as possible, you should leave the first few Generators you find alone.

Sneak up the rest of the stairway, hugging the left wall as you do so. If you spot a guard coming out of the entrance up top, silently take him out with a head shot. If no one appears, move to the top where you will have accomplished your first Primary Objective.

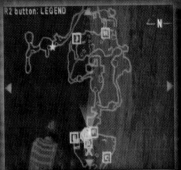

TACMAP

PRIMARY OBJECTIVE 2: LOCATE VAULT

Your next objective is to locate the Vault where the Nukes are being held. If you refer to your TACMAP, you will see that it is very far away, off to the north, deep inside the Cave network. It's not going to be easy to get there but, with skill and patience, you should make it in one piece. Before heading into the Cave entrance, take a moment to peek inside from the cover of the wooden wall. There are at least two guards inside the entrance and possibly three. Watch their movements for a moment, and try to see if there is another one hidden, just out of sight, around the corner of the wall. If you're patient enough, one or two will move into the next room beyond, leaving a solo guard holding his post. Easy pickings for you.

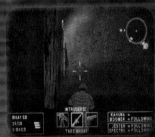   

 You'll find, as soon as you enter the Cave network, that it is a labyrinth of dark and claustrophobic tunnels. To make matters worse, it is riddled with plenty of small alcoves and pitch-black corners, which make for perfect hiding spaces. You will need to go very slow and be very methodical, clearing each area along the way.

Unfortunately, it won't be long until you are spotted. As soon as you are, order Bravo to Fire at Will and get ready for a firefight. Around the corner to the first tunnel is a doorway along the right hand wall. There are many enemies inside this area and you should use the protection of the left wall at its entrance to pick them off as they come screaming out of it. Stay put and take them out until you are fairly certain there are no more coming.

It's likely there are one or two more around the corner inside, so be careful. There also might be one or two more still inside the doorway who haven't yet appeared. This is no time to be careless. Stay alert and go slow. Also be aware of the barrels along the left-hand wall. They are filled with gasoline and are very combustible. A few misplaced shots, from you or an enemy, will send them up in a fiery explosion, taking you with them if you are too close.

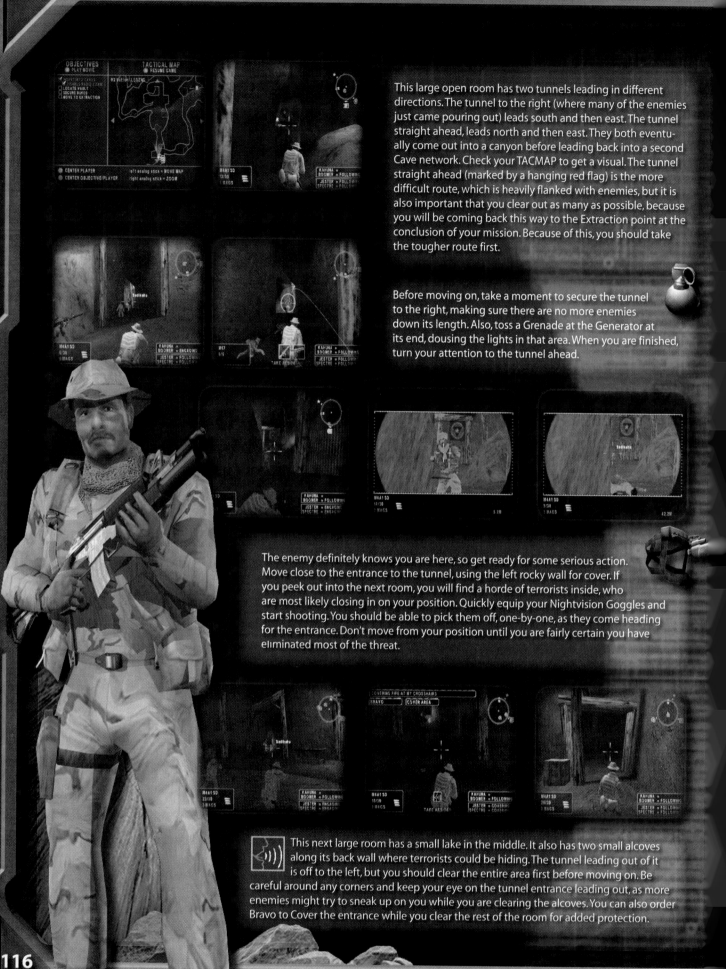

This large open room has two tunnels leading in different directions. The tunnel to the right (where many of the enemies just came pouring out) leads south and then east. The tunnel straight ahead, leads north and then east. They both eventually come out into a canyon before leading back into a second Cave network. Check your TACMAP to get a visual. The tunnel straight ahead (marked by a hanging red flag) is the more difficult route, which is heavily flanked with enemies, but it is also important that you clear out as many as possible, because you will be coming back this way to the Extraction point at the conclusion of your mission. Because of this, you should take the tougher route first.

Before moving on, take a moment to secure the tunnel to the right, making sure there are no more enemies down its length. Also, toss a Grenade at the Generator at its end, dousing the lights in that area. When you are finished, turn your attention to the tunnel ahead.

The enemy definitely knows you are here, so get ready for some serious action. Move close to the entrance to the tunnel, using the left rocky wall for cover. If you peek out into the next room, you will find a horde of terrorists inside, who are most likely closing in on your position. Quickly equip your Nightvision Goggles and start shooting. You should be able to pick them off, one-by-one, as they come heading for the entrance. Don't move from your position until you are fairly certain you have eliminated most of the threat.

This next large room has a small lake in the middle. It also has two small alcoves along its back wall where terrorists could be hiding. The tunnel leading out of it is off to the left, but you should clear the entire area first before moving on. Be careful around any corners and keep your eye on the tunnel entrance leading out, as more enemies might try to sneak up on you while you are clearing the alcoves. You can also order Bravo to Cover the entrance while you clear the rest of the room for added protection.

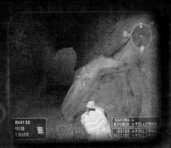

Continue into the next tunnel, using the rocky formations for cover as you go. You will most certainly run into a few more terrorists as you get deeper into the network.

The next small room you come to houses another Generator, some stacked crates, and what is presumably the second Radio Comm, which the terrorists were using to communicate with each other. Use a crate for cover and scan the room for any movement. The exit to the canyon is off to your right, and there is most likely a guard or two somewhere in that general vicinity. Wait them out and pick them off when you get them in your sights.

Take out the Radio and the Generator while you are here as well. Any way you can cripple the Sadikahu is a good thing. Finally, there is a second tunnel, just past the Generator, leading up to an exit above. You can head up there to get a high vantage point and scan the area for terrorists, but it's not necessary or recommended.

Take a moment to scan the area outside from the cover of the exit. You might be able to spot a terrorist or two patrolling the perimeter of the canyon, or up above on the canyon walls. If you find any, pick them off from afar.

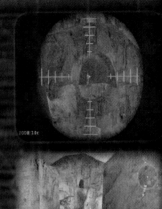

The next Cave entrance is located at Nav point Romeo, off to the southeast. Take a moment to get your bearings and locate it on your TACMAP before heading out.

Use the large rock formations for cover and move from one to the next, as you make your way to the entrance. Be sure to continually scan the canyon floor and walls as you approach the entrance, eliminating any enemies you can find along the way.

TACMAP

SECONDARY OBJECTIVE 2: DISABLE GENERATOR

When you reach the entrance, you will hear the hum of another Generator just beyond. You need to Disable this one and cut off the electricity in the area. This will throw the area into complete darkness, so your Nightvision Goggles will be required to get you through the next area. The Generator is located in the first room, inside the second tunnel entrance, along its back wall to the right. As you enter the Cave, stop and listen for any hostiles in the tunnel beyond. If you hear screaming, that means they are definitely coming for you. Hold your ground and pick them off as they round the corner.

You will find a few more terrorists inside the room with the Generator, use the crates for cover, or the tunnel wall, and neutralize them before Disabling it. A well-thrown Grenade will do the trick.

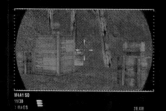

You still have to locate the Vault, which is somewhere down the next tunnel, off to the north. Equip your Nightvision Goggles and head through into the next small room to the right. The room is filled with crates and barrels, and also has a few nooks and crannies, making it hard to spot any hiding enemies with your limited range. Go slow, and clear the room before moving on. There is also a second tunnel, leading up and back outside to the canyon to the left. There is no need to head up this way, as it is a dead end.

When the room is secure, continue into the next tunnel, straight ahead to the north. This cramped area is filled with more crates, making it hard to see what's beyond. Be prepared. There is likely a guard hiding on the other side of the crates to the left. Don't let him ambush you. Peek around and quickly take him out before he has a chance to react.

The tunnel beyond leads upwards, and you can be assured that there are more enemies inside. Caution plays an important role here. If you can wait them out, they will most likely come for you, giving you the ability to pick them off as they appear above. There are at least two that will come from above.

A small room with more crates (and more hiding spaces) waits beyond. If you were patient, it should be empty. If not, be careful and check the corners, as well as behind each crate, for any lingering hostiles. The tunnel beyond continues at a downward slope.

As you move along, you will be privy to Al-Qadi touting much bravado regarding his cause. He knows the Americans are here (that's you), and he's willing to go all the way and detonate the Nukes for his cause. You can't let that happen. Locating the Vault and Securing the Nukes are your highest priority.

When you come down the slope, you will find a lit room. This is the entrance to the Vault. If you are quiet enough, you should be able to sneak up to the wooden blockade without alerting Al-Qadi and his goons to your presence. You can un-equip your Nightvision Goggles to give you a wider range of sight, and prepare to Secure the Nukes. Your Primary Objective should be complete.

TACMAP

PRIMARY OBJECTIVE 3: SECURE NUKES

In order to Secure the Nukes, you will have to eliminate all of the guards protecting the Vault. From your vantage point, you should be able to lean and peek around the wooden wall and locate three to four hostiles. Pick them off if possible, or let them come to you if time allows.

You will inadvertently cause the Sadikahu to arm one of the Nukes, although without a visual, you won't know which one it is. The correct one will have a flashing red light while the other will be green. The two Nukes are located in opposite areas of the Vault, in east and west alcoves. Once they are armed, you will have a paltry one minute and one second to find and disarm the correct one. The countdown timer will appear in the right-hand corner of your screen.

PRIMARY OBJECTIVE 4: DISARM NUKE

TACMAP

Now that the Nuke has been armed, you will have to throw caution to the wind. Make sure you have enough ammunition and, if you are down to one magazine, grab a fallen enemy's rifle.

Quickly verify that you have eliminated the threat inside the first room of the Vault and then move on. There is an intersection straight ahead to the north, with the two Nukes at different ends. The one to the right is closer, so that should be your first destination.

While you are in a rush, you still should be very careful when you approach the alcoves. You will probably encounter a guard hidden somewhere inside, most likely hidden in a corner. Take him out quickly and then check the Nuke.

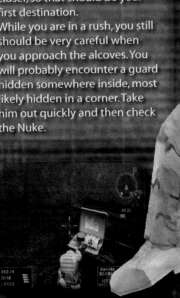

 If you are lucky, the first one will be flashing red. If it is, approach it and Disarm it by pressing the Action (✗) button when the "Disarm Nuke" icon appears. If it's green, quickly make your way to the second Nuke down the other side of the tunnel.

Disarming will take approximately 20 seconds — not much time, so make every one count. You will have to rely on the rest of your SEAL team members to hold their own while you are taking care of the Nuke.

When you have finished disarming the Nuke, make sure you have cleared the rest of the Vault, eliminating any leftover enemies inside. When you have, you will have also completed Primary Objective 3.

PRIMARY OBJECTIVE 5: RESET NUKE

The Nukes can't be left behind, as they are still very dangerous if left in the wrong hands. They also can't be transported due to their completely unstable nature. The only way to get rid of these bad boys is to reset one of them, in essence re-arming it, and then hightail it out of there before the bomb blows. Once one is re-set, you will have seven minutes to head to the extraction zone, which is located way back near the insertion point at Nav point Delta.

Pick a Nuke, it doesn't matter which (although the one on the right side of the Vault is closer to the exit — every second counts), and Reset it by pressing the Action (✗) button when the "Nuke Defuse/Arm" icon appears. 20 seconds later, you have just re-armed a nuclear bomb. It's time to move!

PRIMARY OBJECTIVE 6: MOVE TO EXTRACTION

You have seven minutes to make your way back to the Extraction zone at Nav point Delta. If you quickly refer to your TACMAP, the Extraction zone is marked by a large flashing "X." Even though you have very limited time to extract from the mission, you can't be too careless, as the remaining terrorists are moving toward your location. Head out of the Vault and toward the canyon exit to the west, and use caution around every corner as you go. When you get to the darkened portions of the tunnels, remember to equip your Nightvision Goggles.

Also, continually check your TACMAP to confirm you are on the correct course. You don't have time to waste and getting lost or turned around is not an option.

You'll likely encounter the first of many terrorists as you get close to the canyon exit. Remember to move quickly but cautiously, using the environment for cover as you go.

 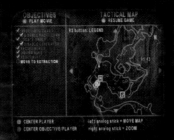 

When you get outside, head to the left, toward the southwest corner of the canyon. The second tunnel entrance is located in the corner, which will provide a quicker and more direct route. Once again, refer to your TACMAP to get a bearing on its location. Be careful when you get to the corner leading to the tunnel's entrance, as you'll most likely encounter a group of guards waiting to ambush you. Quickly mow them down and move on — there is no time for elegant head shots.

Equip your Nightvision Goggles when you get to the tunnel entrance and head inside. You should quickly come to the small room where you destroyed the very first Generator earlier in the mission. Be careful. There is definitely a guard waiting for you inside, as well as another down the tunnel beyond and to the right.

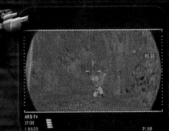

When you get through the next tunnel, take a left and you will find yourself facing the first Cave entrance. Just beyond are the stairs which will lead you down to the Extraction zone. You should have cleared the threat, and can run the rest of the way. When all of your team makes it into the zone, you will have completed your mission with time to spare. A few seconds after your extraction, the Nukes blow, obliterating the Caves and, albeit temporarily, eliminating the threat posed by the Sadikahu.

TURKMENISTAN: OPERATION SERPENT STRIKE
MISSION 12: DEATHBLOW

MISSION OVERVIEW:

"Good work handling the Nukes, team. Now we need to end the Sadikahu threat. Mullah Al-Qadi and his brother, Imad, have retreated to a deserted bombed city in central Turkmenistan. Locate these men and neutralize them. Targets of opportunity are authorized, but focus primarily on elimination of the Al-Qadi brothers."

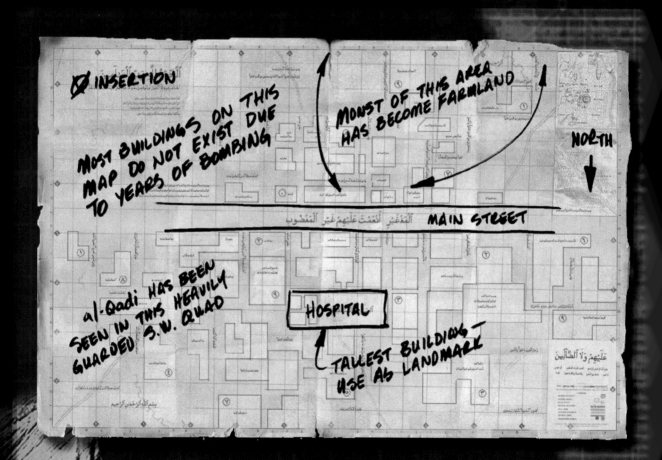

OBJECTIVES

PRIMARY OBJECTIVES
1. ELIMINATE KITTEN
2. ELIMINATE FAT CAT

PRIMARY OBJECTIVE 1: ELIMINATE KITTEN

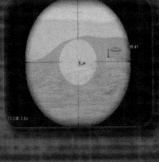

While you were able to eliminate the suitcase Nukes and many Sadikahu trainees, it turns out that Mullah Al-Qadi (code named "Fat Cat") and his brother Imad Al-Qadi (code named "Kitten") have escaped and are on the run. You need to do everything in your power to intercept the terrorist leaders before they can rendezvous with an escape aircraft that could take them out of the country and to safety.

HQ gives us no more than 20 minutes to find and eliminate the Al-Qadi brothers, who are in separate locations in the city. They are also mobile, meaning that they won't be staying put in one place for too long. Since you have backed the Sadikahu into a corner, expect a fierce and savage fight.

Right off the bat, order Bravo to Fire at Will, and then head due west. The path laid out on the TACMAP leads through a swath of the blown out city to the crumbling two-story building that "Kitten" is reportedly housed in. You can try to follow the path, but it is riddled with enemies on all sides who will aggressively attack you with everything they've got.

Instead, continue heading west, toward the broken down wall, stopping every few seconds to eliminate any enemies you can get in your sights. Listen to Able and Bravo call out enemy positions and try to aid them in the fight.

You will definitely encounter at least five or six enemies as you progress.

When you get close to the broken down wall, you'll find an exposed sewage tunnel to your right, located at Nav point Echo on your TACMAP. Wait a moment or two for your fellow SEAL team members to catch up with you (eliminating any hostiles you can spot in the meantime), and then head down into the tunnel.

If you refer to your TACMAP, you'll notice that the tunnel leads straight to the marked building where "Kitten" is stationed. The tunnel branches to the left a little past the midpoint.

If you continue all the way to the end of the tunnel, you will have to climb out, leaving you vulnerable to enemy fire while you are pulling yourself up. Instead, take the left branch of the tunnel, shooting down any enemies you might find as you make your way out.

When you come to the exit, take a few seconds to sweep the area, and try to locate and eliminate any enemies who might be in the general area. If it looks all clear, take an immediate right and climb up the small hill.

You will find yourself in the remains of a bombed out building. Go through the doorway straight ahead to the east, and you will be directly in front of "Kitten's" building.

Before moving in on the building where "Kitten" is located, scan its upper and lower floors for any hostile movement. The more you can eliminate now, the less you will have to deal with when you move in. Don't waste too much time though, as every second that ticks by means another second the Al-Qadi brothers can use to escape.

As soon as you catch your breath, make a dash for "Kitten's" building, heading left toward the opening in the wall. Once inside, use caution and scan the lower level for any hostile movement. You have to find the staircase leading up to the second story, as that's where you'll find "Kitten."

There is a pathway down the middle of the building, leading to all of the open rooms. Take a right at the pathway, and then a right at the next room. The stairs should be directly in front of you.

The second floor is heavily occupied with terrorists protecting "Kitten." Be prepared for heavy resistance. Take out any and all enemies you encounter and head up to the second floor.

You'll find "Kitten" in one of the rooms up-stairs. As soon as he sees you, he will run. He can be identified by his long beard and grey tunic. Eliminate all of his guards, and then quickly finish him off. Don't let him get away.

PRIMARY OBJECTIVE 2: ELIMINATE FAT CAT

TACMAP

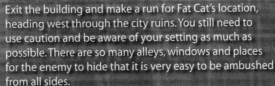

Intel puts Mullah Al-Qadi ("Fat Cat") in a second building west of your position. Locate the general area on your TACMAP and then prepare to move out. It's possible one or two of your SEAL teammates are seriously injured. You can't worry about their safety for the moment, but you will make sure everyone of you makes it out of the area. SEALs never leave a man behind.

Exit the building and make a run for Fat Cat's location, heading west through the city ruins. You still need to use caution and be aware of your setting as much as possible. There are so many alleys, windows and places for the enemy to hide that it is very easy to be ambushed from all sides.

Continually refer to your TACMAP if you become disori-entated or need to check your position. The building you are looking for is a three story structure at the west end of the city.

When you approach the building, take a left down the street in front of it. Instead of entering the building directly, enter the smaller building to the left of it. This building has a makeshift bridge connecting one structure to the next.

Once inside the small building, take the stairs directly to the left of the doorway. When you get to the second floor, take a right and then head for the second set of stairs, which lead to the roof. Take a quick second before heading up to scan the building across the way. If you can take out a few enemies quickly, all the better.

On the roof you will find the bridge leading to Fat Cat's building. Eliminate any enemies blocking your way, and then go across.

Like the structure where you found Kitten, this bombed out building is a maze of small rooms, and Fat Cat could be in any one of them. Search each one until you find him and then chase him down. He will also have guards protecting him and he will run when spotted. It's imperative you don't let him escape. Eliminate any hostiles around him and then take him out before he gets away. When he goes down, you have completed the mission and your support Helo arrives to extract you from the area. Watch for any last second hostiles that might take you down before it can arrive. Mission accomplished!

ONLINE PLAY:

While the single player missions are a huge part of SOCOM: U.S. Navy SEALs, there is also the multiplayer component, which lets you get online and join forces to compete against other players over the Internet (In order to access the multiplayer mode and play online, you must have Sony's Network Adapter and a Broadband Cable or DSL connection to the Internet.) Since every player has their own playing style, this section of the guide offers up some general tools and strategies to help transform you from an online rookie into a multiplaying master.

GETTING ONLINE:

The SOCOM instruction manual offers step-by-step information for getting online. Please refer to it for a more detailed description. Below are the basics for getting you up and running.

LOGGING ON:

You can access the Online Mode from the Main Menu screen. Choose "Online" and then "Login." The next screen you see will be the Connection screen. Using the On-Screen Keyboard, enter your Player Name and Password and then select "Connect." After registering your name, read the User Agreement and select "Yes" if you agree to the terms. This will bring up the SOCOM Online screen.

THE SOCOM ONLINE SCREEN:

The SOCOM Online screen is where you can check out any News or Messages of the day, navigate through the list of available Briefing Rooms, view your SOCOM Online ranking, create and manage Clans, and access the Online Options screen. To quickly join a game, either choose "Autoplay" or "Briefing Rooms," which will take you directly to a Game Lobby. The Game Lobby screen is where you will prepare for battle before heading out. From here, you can access the Armory and switch teams (choosing either SEALs or Terrorists), then head out onto the battlefield.

SPECIFIC STRATEGIES:

There are three types of multiplayer games in SOCOM: Suppression, Extraction and Demolition. Each game type has its own set of specific goals and strategies, although, if you want to really excel at all of them, teamwork and communication are the keys to victory. Below are a set of strategies you can employ that should give you the tactical advantage.

DEMOLITION:

In the Demolition Mode, your goal is to find a Bomb located somewhere within the confines of the environment, secure it, then plant it at the other team's camp. Of course, as soon as you grab the bomb you will be a major target, and will have to stay alive long enough to plant and guard it until it blows up.

STRATEGIES:

Rugby: One strategy is to think of Demolition like a game of Rugby, with the bomb being the ball. In this strategy, you split up your team into smaller groups, leaving one group behind to set up a perimeter and provide cover for your own camp, while the other group goes for the bomb. As soon as you have possession of the bomb, you make a formation behind the team member who has possession, letting him take the lead while the other team members follow from behind. This way, if the team member with the bomb gets eliminated, there is someone right behind him that can pick up the bomb and move on before the enemy can react and grab it.

Kamikaze: Another strategy is to have a lone man grab the bomb, kamikaze-style, while the other team members create a diversion. You can use your other team members to lure the opposition to their location, by either creating noise (throwing smoke grenades and firing shots), or movement (moving out into the open and running in a zig-zag motion). While they are distracting and baiting the enemy, one or two of your team will head for the bomb, secure it, then make for the enemy camp.

TIPS:

When you have possession of the bomb, always enlist another team member's help to guard you while you head for the enemy's camp. This will not only ensure that they will be able to recover it if you are killed, but they can also provide cover for you while you are planting it. It takes approximately five-to-seven seconds to plant and arm the bomb, leaving you vulnerable to enemy fire while you are doing so.

Never leave the bomb once it's been planted. There is a short period of time where an enemy can defuse it if they can get to it quick enough. Always wait it out and guard it until the last possible moment.

SUPPRESSION:

The Suppression Mode is an all-out deathmatch between the SEALs and Terrorists. The team with the most men standing at the end of the five minute match wins the game.

STRATEGIES:

Run & Gun: One strategy is to break off into smaller groups of two, giving you and your team member a better chance of survival by watching each other's backs. Since most of the environments are not "camper-friendly" (meaning there are few places to hide), you should keep moving and constantly scan the perimeter for any hostile movement.

Domination: Another strategy is to keep your entire group together, using the "power in numbers" principle. In doing so, you might lose a few of your teammates but, due to the size of your group, you should be able to overpower any enemies you come across and still come out on top.

Ambush: This strategy works particularly well and is a definite group effort. The idea is to find an open area with cover spots around its perimeter. Have your team members get into cover (hiding in the foliage, crouching behind an object, hugging a corner), then use one person as a decoy to bait the opposition. When they expose themselves, or come looking for you, they will be caught in the crossfire.

TIPS:

Always make sure you have at least one or two snipers on your team and have them take position in strategic, elevated areas, such as hilltops, roofs, sniper towers, etc. Camping is tough, but not impossible. Some maps have thick foliage where a SEAL or Terrorist can get into the prone position and crawl all the way inside, completely hiding their body in the process. In order to see through the brush, just enter the first-person perspective, which places the camera forward a bit, giving you a clear view.

EXTRACTION:

In the Extraction Mode, the Terrorists have captured several hostages and the SEALs must save and extract them from the area.

STRATEGIES:

SEAL: Covert Rescue: One SEAL strategy is to have a two-man team quickly locate and secure the hostages while the other team members provide support through cover fire and elimination, as well as creating havoc to confuse the enemy. Having two team members secure the hostages should give you better odds. If one dies in the attempt, the other will still be able to get to the hostages and move them to safety.

SEAL: Breach Team: Another SEAL strategy is to employ a Breach team to go in ahead of a separate team, and breach and clear the area where the hostages are being held, while the Extraction team waits and provides cover fire. Once the Breach team has secured the area, a second Extraction team can move in and grab the hostages.

Terrorist: Human Shield: If you're playing as the Terrorists, you want to make securing the hostages next to impossible. One way to do so is to use them as human shields. They don't necessarily have to be left in their cell — they can be separated and ordered to follow as well. Once you have them moving, you can put them in between yourself and another terrorist member, making it tough to shoot you without harming the hostage in the process.

Terrorist: Hide the Hostage: Separating the hostages is a huge strategy, as it makes it difficult for the SEALs to locate and extract them. Using this strategy, you can have different team members order a different hostage to follow them, splitting them up and moving each to a remote location somewhere on the map.

TIPS:

For SEALs, try to stagger your team into small groups of two or three, using one to scout and eliminate, a second to follow and breach, a third to extract and a fourth to provide cover. This way, if you lose a team member in the process, one can move up and take the other's place.

Terrorists should always leave one or two members guarding the hostages, making it difficult for the SEALs to get to them without a fight. It's also smart to create a perimeter around the area where the hostages are located, setting up the perfect scenario to ambush them when they go in to secure and extract.

GENERAL STRATEGIES FOR ALL MODES:

- ○ Teamwork! We can't emphasize this enough. Communicating with your team members and using teamwork is the only way you will come out on top. There is very little room for solo tactics and you'll find yourself on the short end of the statistics if you try to fend for yourself. By working together as a team, you can stack the odds in your favor and dominate the opposition.

- ✕ Decoy tactics are encouraged. Using one man as a decoy to draw out the enemy works like a charm. It's smart to have one or two snipers laying in wait while a third moves out into the open. Eventually, an enemy will expose himself as he attempts to take out the decoy, giving his position away in the process.

- △ In levels where you have Nightvision Goggles, you should always have them equipped. Nightvision Goggles push the fog back, magnify your vision and highlight the enemy against the environment, making them much easier to spot and hit.

- □ Using elevation to your advantage is a huge tactic. If you can, it's extremely important that you always get higher then your enemy. This gives you a much better vantage point to shoot from, as well as less of a chance of being spotted. The higher you are, the more advantage you have.

- ○ When shooting at a moving target, always position and lead your cross hairs ahead of the enemy, trying to predict the exact point where it will hit.

- ✕ Using Smoke grenades helps provide you with cover, as well as confuses the enemy. We recommend you don't go around any blind corners without tossing a Smoke grenade first.

- △ You can use the third-person camera to your advantage. By manipulating it to see what might be waiting around corners, you can get the edge on any enemies who might be waiting for you.

- □ Use the prone position whenever possible, as it is the toughest position to be hit from. This goes double for snipers, as your aim is much more steady in this position.